Oxford International Primary

4

Science

Student Book

Deborah Roberts
Terry Hudson

Alan Haigh
Geraldine Shaw

Language consultants:
John McMahon
Liz McMahon

OXFORD

Great Clarendon Street, Oxford, OX2 6DP, United Kingdom

Oxford University Press is a department of the University of Oxford. It furthers the University's objective of excellence in research, scholarship, and education by publishing worldwide. Oxford is a registered trade mark of Oxford University Press in the UK and in certain other countries.

British Library Cataloguing in Publication Data

Data available

ISBN 978-1-38-200657-6

7 9 10 8 6

Paper used in the production of this book is a natural, recyclable product made from wood grown in sustainable forests. The manufacturing process conforms to the environmental regulations of the country of origin.

Printed in China by Golden Cup

Acknowledgements

The publisher and authors would like to thank the following for permission to use photographs and other copyright material:

Cover: Artwork by Blindsalida. **Photos: p19(l):** Madlen/Shutterstock; **p19(m):** Roxana Bashyrova/Shutterstock; **p19(r):** koosen/Shutterstock; **p39(a):** Iakov Filimonov/Shutterstock/DAM; **p39(b):** Pu Su Lan/Shutterstock; **p39(c):** Corbis; **p39(d):** Digital Stock/Corbis; **p39(e):** Digital Stock/Corbis; **p44:** Zuzana Randlova/ Dreamstime; **p48(a):** Anne Kitzman/Shutterstock; **p48(b):** Weerachai chandang/ Shutterstock; **p48(c):** Joseph Sohm/Shutterstock; **p48(d):** Sonia Bonet/Shut- terstock; **p48(e):** Sonia Bonet/Shutterstock; **p50:** Nature Picture Library/Alamy Stock Photo; **p54(a):** DoublePHOTO studio/Shutterstock; **p54(b):** Vibrant Image Studio/Shutterstock; **p54(c):** JRP Studio/Shutterstock; **p54(d):** Sky Light Pictures/ Shutterstock; **p54(e):** Olha Rohulya/Shutterstock; **p61:** Cool Vector Maker/Shut- terstock; **p85:** Quincy Russell, Mona Lisa Production/Science Photo Library; **p91(l):** Richard Codington/Alamy Stock Photo; **p91(r):** Jim Cumming/Alamy Stock Photo; **p109:** Chaichan Ingkawaranon/Alamy Stock Photo; **p128:** Monty Rakusen/Cultura/Getty Images; **p134:** Lourens Smak/Alamy Stock Photo.

Artwork by Q2A Media Services Pvt. Ltd.

Every effort has been made to contact copyright holders of material reproduced in this book. Any omissions will be rectified in subsequent printings if notice is given to the publisher.

Contents

Contents

How to Use this Book

This Student Book for Oxford International Primary Science forms part of your science lessons for this year. Your teacher will introduce the ideas through whole-class activities, then you will explore them in more detail using this book, before all coming back together to discuss what you have learned. Find out more at: www.oxfordprimary.com/international-science

Structure of the book

This book is divided into five units plus a *Being a Good Scientist* introduction and a picture Glossary:

Being a Good Scientist
Unit 1 Solids, Liquids and Gases
Unit 2 Habitats
Unit 3 Digestion and Food Chains
Unit 4 Electricity
Unit 5 Sounds
Glossary

Each unit covers a different strand of science. You will need a science notebook to write in and to record your investigation results and conclusions.

Being a good scientist

To be a good scientist you need to be curious and ask questions. This section will help you think about how to develop your scientific skills to work like a scientist.

What you will find in each unit

There are three types of lessons:
Wow introduces each unit's scientific ideas and key words. It tells you what you will learn in the unit and lets you discuss what you already know.
Focused lessons cover the scientific knowledge and skills you need to learn this year.
In **What have I learned?** you review your learning and show your teacher what you have learned about the unit.

What you will find in the lessons

Although each lesson is unique, they have common features:

The words on the Wow pages are included in the picture glossary at the back of the book. You can add your own notes for each word.

Key words
pollution
turbidity
Gives you the key words for the lesson.

In this lesson you will learn how to use identification keys. Tells you what you will learn in the lesson.

Questions to help you talk to each other and share ideas about the science you are learning and the investigations you do.

Practical and research activities to investigate and report on science topics. Sometimes your teacher will ask you to use different equipment, which is available in school. They may also ask you to carry out a test in a different way, to make sure you are safe.

Stretch zone Challenges you to take your learning further.

Key idea Summarises what you have learned.

Additional features

Think back Reminds you what has been covered before.

Science fact Interesting and amazing science facts.

Highlights the skills needed to be a good scientist.

Important notes about how to stay safe.

Teacher's Guide

There is a Teacher's Guide to help your teacher to work out the resources needed and to offer alternative activities and approaches.

Workbook

At the bottom of each page in this book is a link to a Workbook, where you can record your work and get extra practice to do in your lesson or at home.

Being a Good Scientist

Science is the study of the world around us. To be a good scientist you need to be curious and ask questions. This section will help you think about how to develop your scientific skills to work like a scientist.

Scientists look carefully at the world to explain why things happen and to guess if things may happen. Science is used to develop new technologies. It also helps us know more about health and diseases. This means we can develop medicines and machines to keep people healthy.

You will have to make decisions about the type of scientific investigations you should be doing and which observations you should be carrying out. You will need to bring all of your skills together to plan and carry out fair tests and to record and present your findings.

The diagram shows the steps you can take to plan and carry out investigations like a scientist.

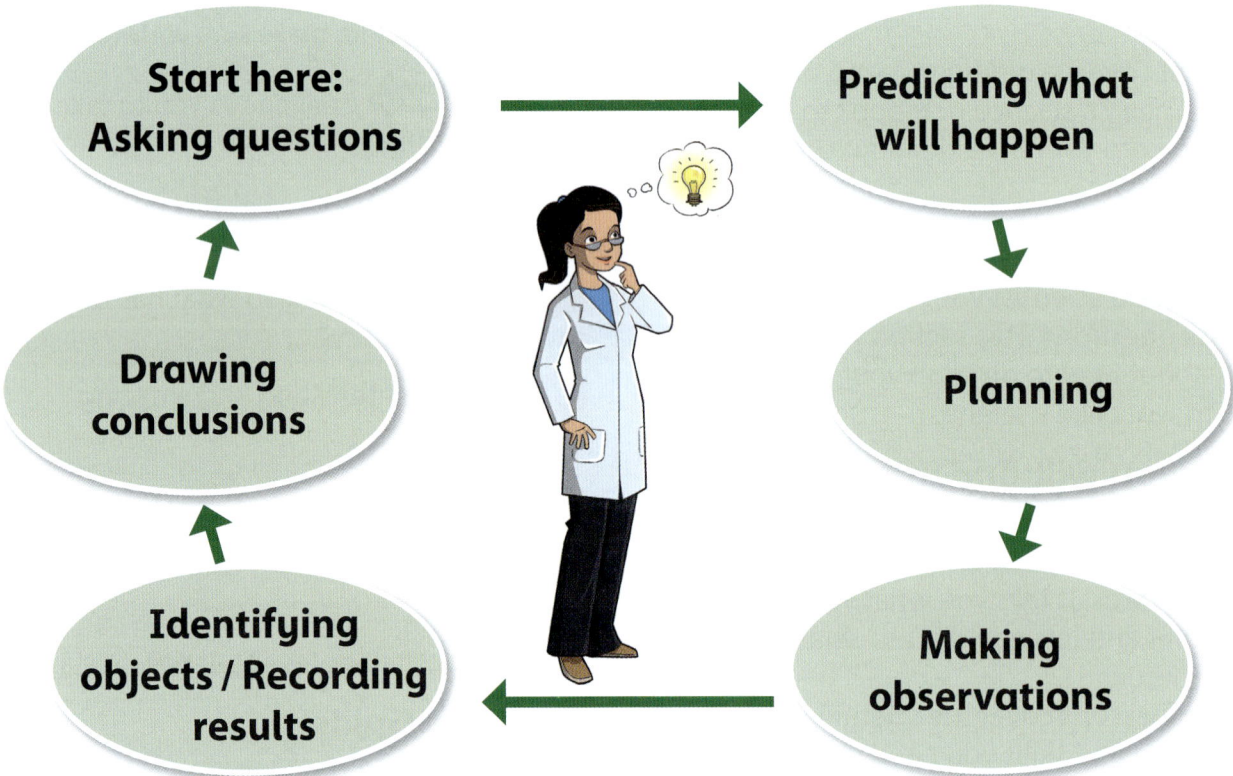

Learning to be a scientist allows you to develop scientific skills such as observing (looking), measuring and recording. It helps you to notice patterns in the things you observe and to sort things into groups. It also helps you to test your own ideas about how the world works.

Asking questions

Scientists ask questions about the world around them. This is called scientific enquiry.

A good way to start is to think of questions that start with words such as 'which', 'what', 'why', 'how', 'do' and 'does'. Your questions should lead you towards planning an investigation or carrying out research to find out more about a subject.

> Does the substance have a fixed volume?

> Does it have a fixed shape?

> Think of your own questions to ask about materials. Think about different properties the materials can have.

The questions you ask will give you a good start to your investigation.

Questions can also come out of the results of an investigation. For example, when investigating materials you might observe that materials changed when they were cooled or heated. What questions would these results make you think about?

That is why the investigative process is shown in a circle. Each investigation can lead to new questions to investigate.

Predicting what will happen

Next, scientists try to work out what will happen. Scientists call this a prediction.

They need to talk about their ideas and think about what they already know about a topic. You might have already learned something about the question you are trying to answer. Scientists usually know something before they make predictions.

Use what you know about melting to help you think about this question.

> What would you observe if you warmed a cube of ice on a windowsill?

> Do you think the ice would change?
>
> What did you think about to help you decide?

As a scientist, you draw on your previous experiences to help. Think about when you have seen ice and water. You could also think about how water can be changed into different forms in a kitchen. This makes your prediction much better than a guess. It is based on scientific knowledge and evidence.

Scientists often use **models** to represent objects or the way things work. Models help scientists to think about new ideas or things that cannot be seen. For example, your classmates can model how particles in a solid and liquid change when materials melt and freeze. Scientists use models to make predictions and to explain observations.

Planning an investigation

Scientists plan what they are going to do. They always discuss their plans before they start. This helps to check that the plan will work.

You will be encouraged to set up what are called **comparative tests**. This is when you design an investigation to compare different things. For example, you might want to compare the insects and plants in two different areas.

How are the students investigating plants and insects?

Why are they using small quadrats or squares?

It is important that an investigation is a **fair test**. Scientists make their investigations fair by following some simple rules:

- They think about what to keep the same.
- They think about what to change.

For example, when investigating different habitats, you should survey the same amount of ground to make a fair comparison.

If you surveyed a large area in one place and a small area in another place, then it would not be a fair test to compare which has the most plants or insects.

Scientists think about the **equipment** they need. They make a list and make sure everything is available. For example, if you are going to survey the number of insects in an area you might make a list like this:

quadrat
pooter
net
measuring tape
hand lens
small collecting pot

Science fact

Scientists do not always plan their own investigations. Sometimes they follow other scientist's plans. This is why it is very important to make the plans clear.

Sometimes it is not possible to plan an investigation to answer your questions. For example, if you want to know about insects high up in trees or on a cliff face, you will not be able to reach there to observe them. It would not be safe. You will have to use other sources of information such as the internet, books and magazines. These are called **secondary sources of information**.

When have you used secondary sources to find out more about science?

What were they?

How did you use them?

Making observations

Scientists use their observation skills during investigations.

What are the different senses you can use when observing investigations? Write a list.
Why do you have to be careful when using these senses?

Scientists do not just observe investigations when they have a bit of time. They plan carefully to make observations at the right times. They use computers, data loggers and other devices, such as smartphones and electronic scales, to help them to take accurate measurements.

Some of the pieces of equipment you will use this year are shown below.

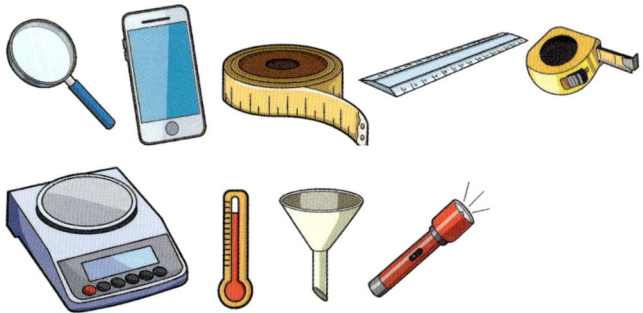

Scientists are very careful to use standard units to record their results. Standard units allow people from all over the world to understand the results. For example, when measuring plant heights, they would use millimetres or centimetres. They would not use grams or degrees.

Which standard units would you use to measure: a) temperature, b) the distance between villages, c) the amount of flour needed in a recipe?

Good scientists take a measurement more than once. This is to make sure they have not made any mistakes. They then find out the average for their readings. The example below shows the results of a habitat survey.

Animal	Number of animals found under a stone			
	Count 1	Count 2	Count 3	Average
woodlouse	2	8	5	
ant	3	1	2	
worm	1	1	1	

What should the average readings be for each animal? Which animal was the most common under the stone? Why was it useful to not just take the first readings?

To identify objects you may use a key. This is a diagram with simple questions. As you answer the questions it moves you closer to the object you are trying to identify.

Look at this invertebrate key.

Identify a millipede, using the key.

Why are keys useful?

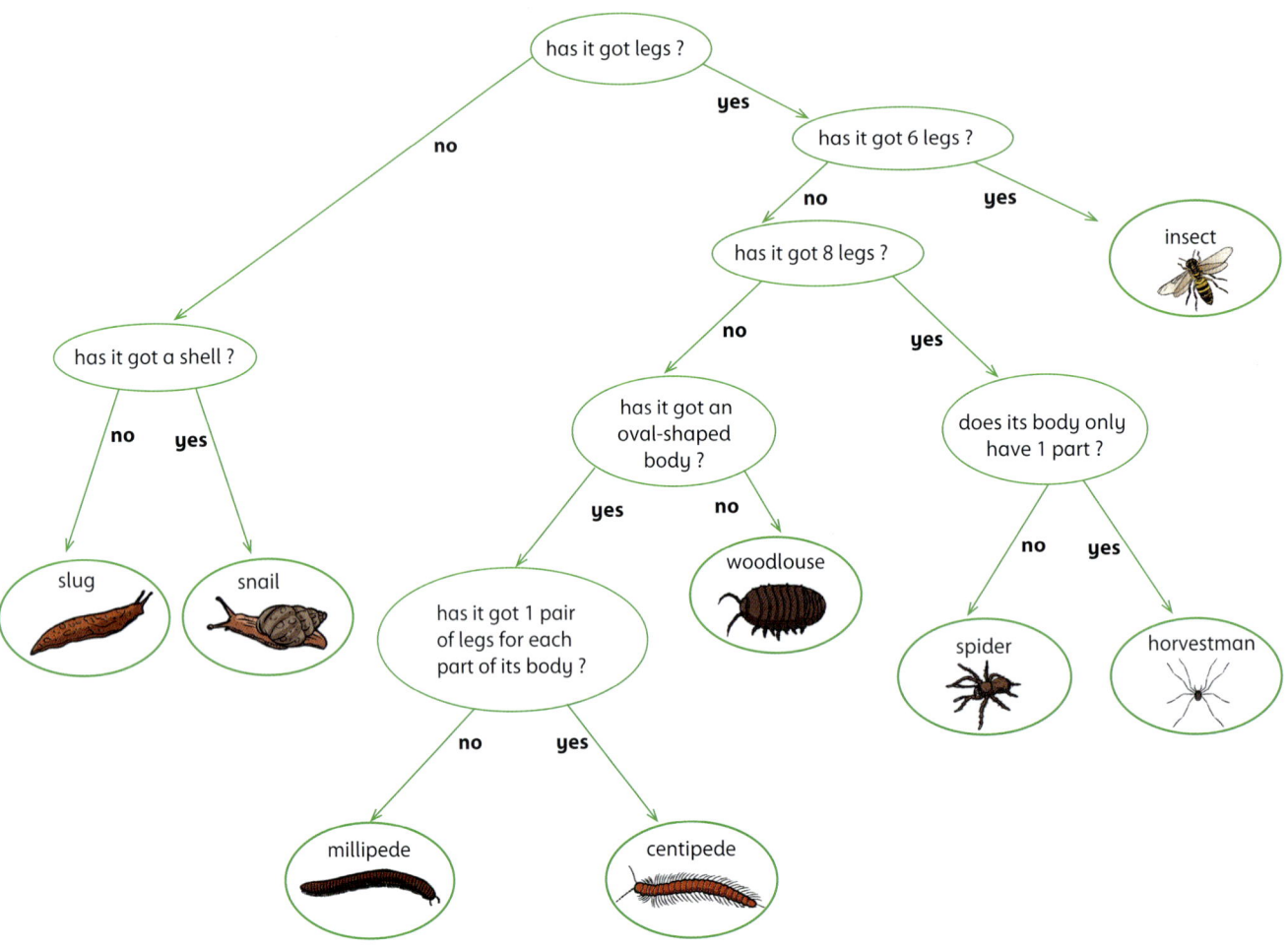

Recording results

Scientists write down or record what they have found from their observations and measurements. This helps them to see patterns or to sort things into groups.

You will need to use your results to draw conclusions. This is the next part of the investigation process. This means that if you do not record your results carefully, you may not be able to make the most sensible conclusions. There are lots of different ways to record results.

Tables

One way to record results is to complete a table.

You could use a table like this one to record how quickly 100 cm³ of water will evaporate at different temperatures. The water should be poured into identical shallow dishes.

Temperature (°C)	Time taken for the water to evaporate (minutes)
20	180
30	170
40	150
50	100
60	70
70	30

Look at the table. Answer these questions with your partner.

Which temperature shows the fastest evaporation time?

Describe any patterns you can see in the results.

Name another thing that needs to be kept the same in this investigation.

Charts

Results from tables can be shown as charts or graphs.

This chart shows the results of the evaporation investigation.

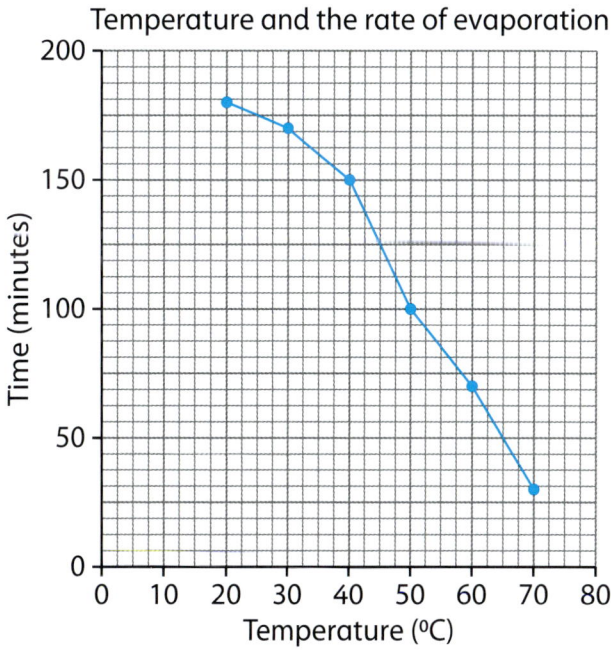

Temperature and the rate of evaporation

The time it takes for the water to evaporate (the measurement that changes) is plotted from bottom to top on this chart. This is the y-axis.

The temperatures investigated (the measurement that is agreed at the start) are plotted along the bottom on this chart. This is the x-axis.

Do you think the chart on page 11 is easier or harder to read from than the table of results?

Predict the time it would take for water to evaporate from the dishes at 10°C and 80°C.

Using charts can sometimes make it easier to see patterns in the results. We can also extend the lines of a graph to help us to make predictions.

Drawings, photographs and videos

You have worked with scientific drawings before. Remember they are not like the pictures you paint.

Scientific drawings are much simpler

Scientists also use modern technology to take photographs and video clips of their investigations and results.

Photographs show a lot of detail

This is a very accurate way to record results. This level of detail would not be possible without using a camera.

Filming allows us to see things that may be impossible to see in person.

Scientists can see tiny details, such as how a water droplet behaves, by slowing down a film

How could you use a camera or video recorder to observe what happens as water is heated?

Drawing conclusions

The last stage of an investigation is when scientists look at their results carefully. It is at this stage that they make sense of their results. They work out if the results have helped them to answer their investigation question.

The questions they might ask are:

Can I *see* any patterns?

Are any results unusual?

Was my prediction correct?

Scientists also link their conclusions to bigger scientific ideas. For example, if they are thinking about the animals they have found in a habitat, they will link this to the foods the animals eat and what eats them. They will also think about other factors, such as how much water there is and how warm or cold it is.

After completing an investigation, a good scientist will do three things:

1 Think about how accurate the results are

They will try to work out ways to improve their investigation.

2 Report the findings to others

They do this by talking to others, writing a report or making a display. This might be a poster or a computer presentation. They may include models.

Scientists are very careful to use the correct scientific language. This makes their ideas much clearer. They also plan their reports and presentations to match their audience. For example, if they are talking to people who are not scientists, they will not include as much detail as they would in a scientific paper.

3 Think about any new questions that the investigation has raised

For example, if they studied different animals in a habitat, could that be linked to the different plants that also live there?

It is useful to fill out an investigation planning form. This sets out all the stages of your investigation. It helps you to remember everything you need to think about. Your teacher can give you one of these.

1 Solids, Liquids and Gases

In this unit you will:

- compare and group materials into solids, liquids and gases
- investigate how materials change when they are heated and cooled
- measure and research how different materials melt and freeze at different temperatures
- observe that water turns into steam when it is heated and that it turns back into water when it is cooled
- explore the water cycle.

The diver is swimming beneath the ice and breathing air from a bottle.

What solid, liquid and gas can you see in the photograph?

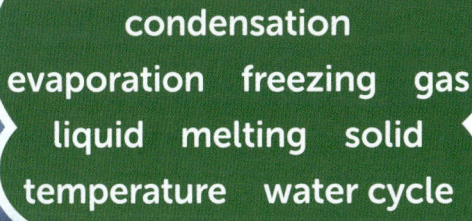

condensation
evaporation   freezing   gas
liquid   melting   solid
temperature   water cycle

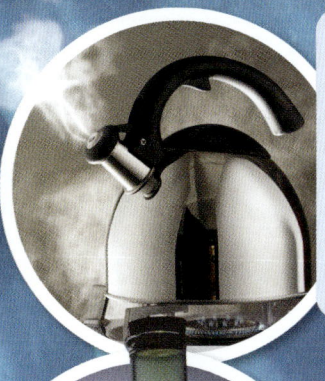

Look at the photograph of a kettle.

What is the white cloud?

Do you think the kettle is hot or cold? Why?

There are gases in the air all around us but we cannot see them. They are transparent. Some gases do have colour. These are easier to see.

Look at the gas in the photograph. How is it different from solids such as ice and wood?

Chlorine gas is green

Science fact

We live on a watery planet. 70% of the surface of the Earth is water.

■ For more activities, go to Workbook 4 pages 14–15

Are they solids, liquids or gases?

In this lesson you will compare and group materials into solids, liquids or gases.

Key words

gas

liquid

matter

property

pure

solid

state

 Look at the photograph.

Discuss any solids, liquids and gases that you can see.

Decide whether 1, 2 and 3 are solid, liquid or gas.

Everything around you that takes up space is called matter. The chair we sit on, the water we drink and the air we breathe are all made of matter. Sound and light are not matter. Materials are made from matter. Materials can be made of one thing or a mixture of things. If a material is only made from one thing, it is pure and is called a substance. Water and salt are substances.

Grouping materials into solid, liquid or gas

You are going to compare and group some materials.

1 Copy this table into your notebook.

Material	Solid	Liquid	Gas
blood			
carbon dioxide			
copper			
milk			
oxygen			
paper			
petrol			
plastic			
wood			

2 With your partner, decide if the material is a solid, liquid or gas. Colour the box, as shown in the first row.

3 Make up some rules to help you identify the solids. Then do the same for the liquids and the gases.

Science fact

Even hard metals such as iron can be liquid. Solid iron needs to be heated to 1538°C to make it change to liquid iron.

16

■ For more activities, go to Workbook 4 page 16.

Properties of materials

The properties of a material describe the way it looks, feels and behaves. We use properties to show whether a material is a solid, liquid or a gas.

We call solids, liquids and gases the three states of matter.

Look at the properties in the table. Did you include any of these in your own rules in the last activity?

Property	Solid	Liquid	Gas
Does it have a fixed volume?	Yes	Yes	No. It changes to fill the container
Does it have a fixed shape?	Yes	No. It changes to fit the shape of the container	No. It changes to fill all of the container's shape
How dense is it?	Very dense	Dense	Not dense
How easy is it to squash?	Hard to squash	Hard to squash	Easy to squash
Does it flow?	No	Yes	Yes

Identifying solids, liquids and gases

You are going to use the properties from the table above to identify solids, liquids and gases.

Your teacher will give you some materials to identify.

1 Check each material and group all the solids together.

2 Then group all the liquids together, and then the gases.

3 Record your results in a table in your notebook.

   Highlight the names of any solids in green.

   Highlight the names of any liquids in blue.

   Highlight the names of any gases in yellow.

Be a scientist

Good scientists ask questions and discuss their ideas. Talk about each material before making a decision.

▶ page 7

Key ideas

- The three states of matter are solid, liquid and gas.
- We can decide if materials are solids, liquids or gases by comparing their properties.

17

■ For more activities, go to Workbook 4, page 17.

Particles

In this lesson you will find out that matter can be solid, liquid or gas.

Key words

matter

model

particle

Think back

Look at the photograph. Which container is full of gases? How do you know?

Every material is made up of tiny particles. For example, copper is made from copper particles. The particles in solids, liquids and gases are arranged differently. If there was a microscope powerful enough, we could look at the particles in more detail. We would see that the particles move all the time. We say they are in constant motion. We would also see how the different arrangement helps to explain their properties.

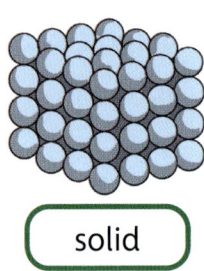

solid

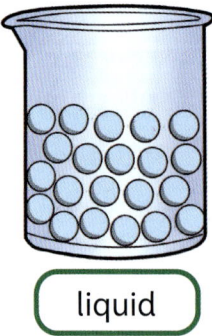

liquid

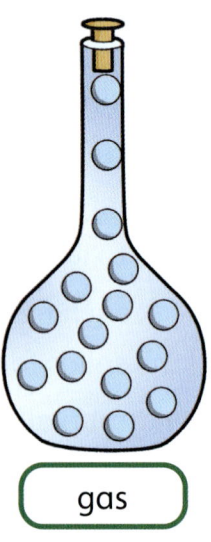

gas

In the solid, the particles are packed closely together. They move but not very much.

In the liquid, the particles are not packed as closely together. They can move a small amount.

In the gas, the particles are far apart. They can move quickly in every direction.

■ For more activities, go to Workbook 4 page 18.

Look at the drawings on page 18 of the particles in a solid, a liquid and a gas. Discuss these questions with your partner.

1 Why do you think solids are hard and have a fixed shape?

2 Why do you think liquids have the same shape as the container and can be poured?

3 Why do you think gases have no fixed shape or volume?

Modelling particles

Everyone in your group will be a particle.

1 Decide how you will arrange yourselves so that you model the particles in a solid.

Once you are arranged, your teacher will say 'change'.

2 Arrange yourselves so that you model the particles in a liquid.

Your teacher will say 'change' once more.

3 Now arrange yourselves so that you model the particles in a gas.

You could do the activity again and ask someone to film it so you can watch yourselves being solids, liquids and gases.

Were you able to move around the most in a solid, a liquid or a gas?

 Stretch zone

Write a plan of how your group could model what happens to particles when water is placed into a freezer.

Key ideas

- All matter is made up of particles that are in constant motion.
- In solids, the particles are closely packed together. They are further apart in liquids and free to move in gases.

■ For more activities, go to Workbook 4 page 19.

Liquids

In this lesson you will find out about liquids.

We know that liquids flow and can be poured. We often pour water from one container (or from the tap) into another container.

Key words

liquid
particle
shape
volume

Which liquids are in these photographs?

What is the volume and shape of liquids?

You are going to investigate what happens when you pour the same amount of water into different shaped containers.

1 Select four different transparent containers.

2 Pour 100 millilitres (ml) of water into each container.

3 Look at the containers carefully and answer these questions with a partner.

- Do some containers look as if they contain more water?

- What shape is the water in each container?

- How easy was it to pour the water?

4 Record your observations in your notebook.

Look at the table on page 17 again. Why did the poured water take on the shape of the bottles?

When people sell liquids they sometimes put them into different shaped bottles. This is so they look attractive, but also so we think we are getting more for our money.

■ For more activities, go to Workbook 4 page 20.

Think back to your investigation. You may have seen containers like these filled with water.

Discuss with your partner.
- Which container looks as if it has the most water?
- Which container looks as if it has the smallest amount of water?
- Look at the measurements. What is the volume of water in each container?

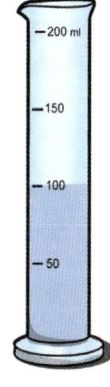

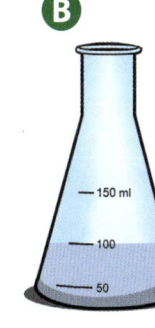

Are powders liquids?

We can pour powders, so does this mean that they are liquids? Let's investigate.

1 Take some sugar cubes. These are solids.

How do you know they are solids?

2 Pour the sugar lumps from one bowl to another.

The sugar lumps poured, but are they liquids?

3 Carefully crush the sugar cubes into very small pieces to make a powder.

4 Pour the powdered sugar from one bowl to another. It pours even better.

The powdered sugar pours, so is it a liquid?

5 Look at the powder with a hand lens or microscope. What do you see? Is the sugar still a solid? Record your observations.

6 Design a small poster to explain why a liquid will pour but solids do not. Use particle drawings.

Science fact

Powders behave like liquids but they are solids.

Key idea

We can pour liquids because the particles are close together but not tightly packed.

■ For more activities, go to Workbook 4 page 21.

Gases

In this lesson you will find out about gases.

Key words

gas

liquid

solid

Think back

Read each sentence. Decide if it describes a solid, a liquid or a gas. Identify the material.

1 I am cold and white. I float on the sea when it is very cold.

2 I am in rain and you can pour me. You can see through me and drink me.

3 I am in the air. You breathe me in to stay alive.

Gases are very important. The atmosphere that surrounds the Earth is a mixture of gases. So the air we breathe is made up of a mixture of the gases oxygen, nitrogen, argon, neon, carbon dioxide and water vapour. Other gases like hydrogen and methane are used for fuels.

At room temperature these are gases but if they are cooled, they become liquids and eventually solids.

You are now going to investigate gases.

Making bubbles

1 Make a circle using thin wire. Leave enough wire to make a handle.

2 Dip your circle into soapy water.

3 Gently blow to make bubbles.

4 Can you make bubbles by moving the circle gently through the air?

5 Investigate to find out if changing the size of the wire circle will change the size of the bubbles.

6 Investigate to find out if changing the shape of the wire will change the shape of the bubbles.

7 Record the results of your investigations.

8 Write a short report of your findings.

■ For more activities, go to Workbook 4 page 22.

Making and testing gases

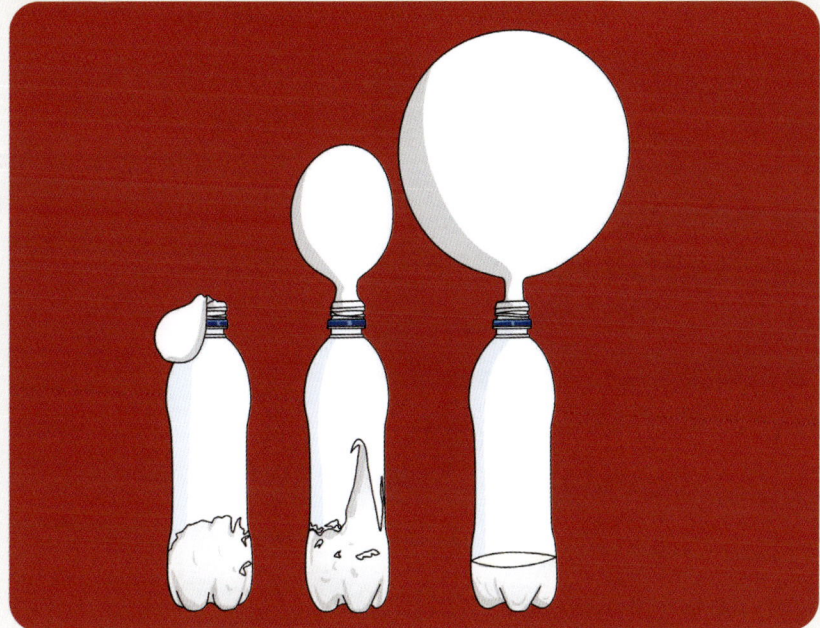

You are going to make a gas called carbon dioxide.

1 Carefully put three small spoons of baking soda into a balloon.

2 Pour vinegar into a small plastic bottle until it is about one-third full.

3 Fit the balloon over the bottle opening. Be careful not to drop the baking soda into the bottle.

4 Hold up the balloon and slowly pour the baking soda into the vinegar. What happens?

Talk about how you know that a gas is being made.

5 Record your investigation and your observations.

6 Squeeze the balloon. Record if it is easy or hard to squash the gas. Explain why. Use the idea of particles to help.

 Stretch zone

Find out the percentages of different gases in the air we breathe. Draw a pie chart to present your findings.

Warning!
Wear goggles when pouring vinegar. Rinse any splashes with water. Discuss why this is important.

Key idea
Gases are easy to squash and spread out to fill their container because their particles are free to move.

■ For more activities, go to Workbook 4 page 23.

Heating materials

In this lesson you will investigate how materials change state when they are heated.

Key words

heating

melting

state

Discuss the photographs with a partner. What is the link between the two photographs?

Tell your partner one example of where you have seen heat in cooking.

Why do we heat some foods?

When we heat materials we add energy to them. The particles start to move faster and move further apart.

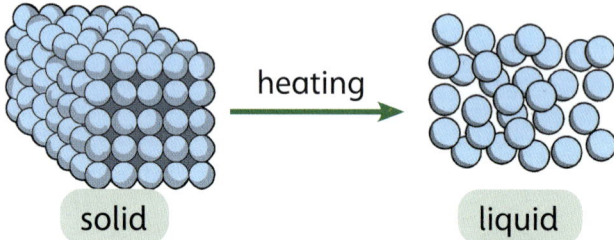

solid   heating   liquid

Modelling the heating of a solid

You are going to act out what happens to the particles of a solid when they are heated.

1 Start with all of the people in your group arranged tightly packed.

2 Now move a little bit more.

3 Stop when you can move freely but all of the particles are still touching.

4 Discuss what happened to the solid as it was heated.

Did the solid change into a liquid or a gas?

■ For more activities, go to Workbook 4 page 24.

How do materials change when we heat them?

You are going to heat some chocolate and observe what happens.

Warning!
Do not touch the hot water or the bowl. Hot water is very dangerous.

1 Put a heatproof bowl inside a metal pan.

2 Put your chocolate in the bowl.

3 Your teacher will pour hot water into the pan so that the bowl is standing in the hot water.

4 Gently stir the chocolate for five minutes.

5 Write a report of your investigation.

Describe what the chocolate looked like before and after you heated it.

Explain when the chocolate was solid and when it was a liquid.

When we heated solid chocolate it changed into liquid chocolate. This is an example of a change of state.

The change from a solid to a liquid is called melting.

Even metals can melt. A lot of heat is needed to make them change from solid metal to liquid metal.

Look at the photograph of the ice cream. Discuss why this is an example of melting.

Very hot liquid metal can be poured

Why is it useful to have melted metals? What can be made from them?

Stretch zone

Research three more examples of solids melting to give a liquid. Make a presentation to share with your class.

Key ideas

- When materials are heated, the particles gain more energy. They start to move faster and further apart.
- Solids can change state into liquids. This is called melting.

■ For more activities, go to Workbook 4 page 25.

Heating liquids

In this lesson you will investigate how water changes state when it is heated.

Key words
boil
evaporate
liquid
melt

Think back

What happens to the particles in a material when it is heated?

Water is a liquid. You have seen water being heated.

Look at the photograph. What do you see when water gets hotter and hotter?

What happens when water boils?

Your teacher will show you what happens when water is heated.

1 Predict what will happen to the water.

2 Observe the water very carefully. Write down what it looked like before it was heated.

3 Record your observations during the heating.

4 Write down what it looked like after it was heated.

5 Was your prediction correct?

6 Write up your observations into a summary of the investigation. Include the following words: heating, particles, liquid, gas.

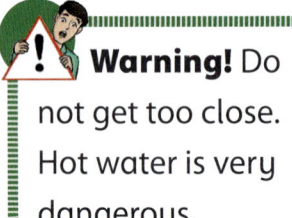
Warning! Do not get too close. Hot water is very dangerous.

When we heat water, the heat gives the water particles energy. The water particles spread out and can turn to gas inside the liquid. This makes bubbles. The water is boiling. The very hot water vapour is called steam.

■ For more activities, go to Workbook 4 page 26.

Evaporation

In warm weather or in a warm room, water particles can escape from the surface of water. The water slowly dries up. The liquid water changes to a gas called water vapour. This is called evaporation.

Can you speed up evaporation?

1 You will be given four pieces of wet cloth.
   - Place one cloth open on a line in the Sun.
   - Place one cloth in a sunny place but folded into a tight ball.
   - Place one cloth open in a shady but windy place.
   - Place one cloth open in a cool place which is a little wet.

2 Design a table and record what happens to the cloths every 10 minutes for an hour.

3 Which cloth dried the quickest?

   Which cloth dried the slowest?

4 Write a short report to explain how to speed up and slow down evaporation.

Discuss what happens to the water in the wet clothes.

Be a scientist

Scientists use tables to record their data. They can then share and present the data with others.

▶ page 11

Stretch zone

Discuss the difference between evaporation and boiling.

Which one happens when a rain puddle dries up?

Key ideas

- When liquid water is heated, it changes state into a gas called water vapour. This is called evaporation.
- When the temperature increases, so does the amount of evaporation.

■ For more activities, go to Workbook 4 page 27.

Investigating melting

In this lesson you will investigate how materials change state when they are heated.

Think back

With a partner think of two examples of each of the following changes of state:

- a solid changing into a liquid
- a liquid changing into a gas.

What are these changes of state called?

Key words

global warming

liquid

melt

solid

state

Global warming

Many scientists believe that global warming is melting the frozen parts of the Earth. The North and South Poles are a long way away, but the melting ice will cause problems for all of us.

Science fact

Global warming is changing the Earth's climate or weather patterns. This is why scientists talk about climate change.

How might the melting of the frozen parts of the Earth affect us?

How might other living things on Earth be affected?

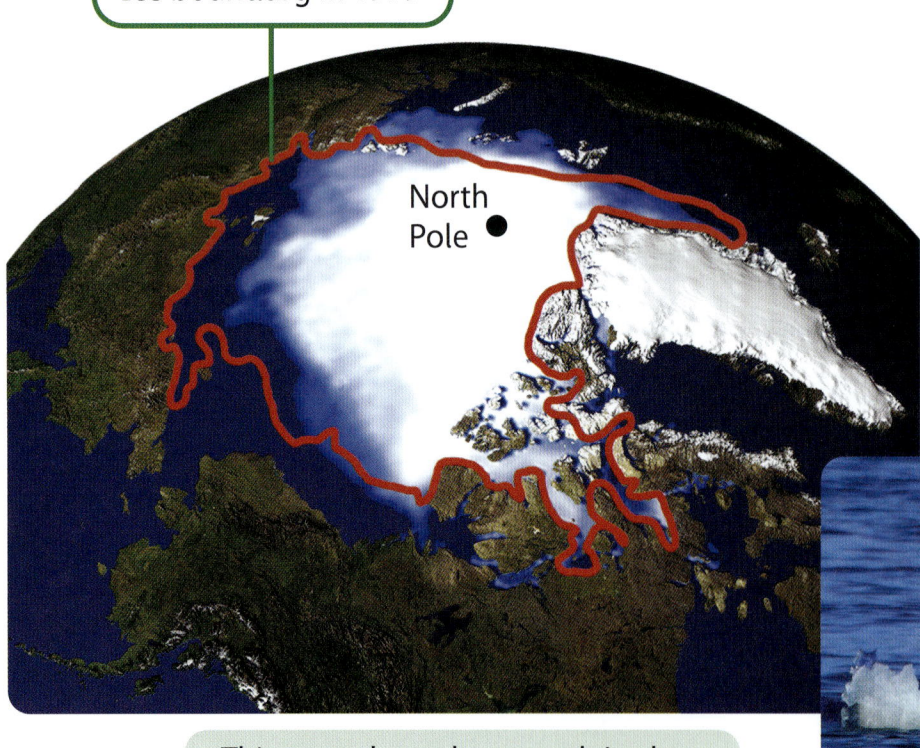

Ice boundary in 1979

North Pole

This map shows how much ice has melted at the North Pole since 1979

■ For more activities, go to Workbook 4 page 28.

How can we slow down melting?

You are going to try to keep ice cubes frozen for as long as possible.

before   during   near the end

1 Why do ice cubes melt? Discuss with your partner.

2 If we do not have a freezer or a refrigerator, how can we slow down the melting?

- Design a plan.
- Try out your ideas and record the results.

3 Share your results with the rest of the class. Discuss which ideas worked the best.

Be a scientist

Remember to make sure your investigation is a fair test.

▶ page 8

Researching climate change

1 Produce an information poster about climate change.

2 Use the internet to find out how climate change is affecting life on Earth. Explain how climate change is making ice change to water in the environment.

3 Include facts, pictures, diagrams and data on your poster.

Key ideas

- When heated, a solid can change state into a liquid. This is called melting.
- Keeping a material cool will slow down how quickly it melts.

Stretch zone

Discuss with a partner one thing people could change to stop or slow down climate change.

■ For more activities, go to Workbook 4 page 29.

Melting and freezing

In this lesson you will find out that materials melt and freeze at different temperatures.

Key words

freeze

melt

reverse

steam

temperature

thermometer

Think back

Water is one of the most common materials on Earth.

What percentage of the Earth's surface is covered by water?

When a solid such as ice is heated, it changes state into a liquid. This process is called melting.

The change in state from liquid to a solid is called freezing. Freezing is the reverse of melting.

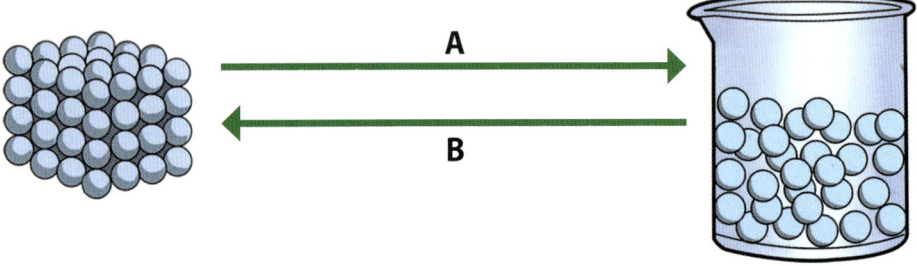

Which arrow shows the change from a liquid to a solid?

What is this process called?

Which arrow shows the melting of a solid? What does the solid become?

Water

Water exists on Earth in all three of its states. It can be ice, water and steam. Water is very important in all of its states.

With a partner, describe two examples of where we can find water in each of its three states.

■ For more activities, go to Workbook 4 page 30.

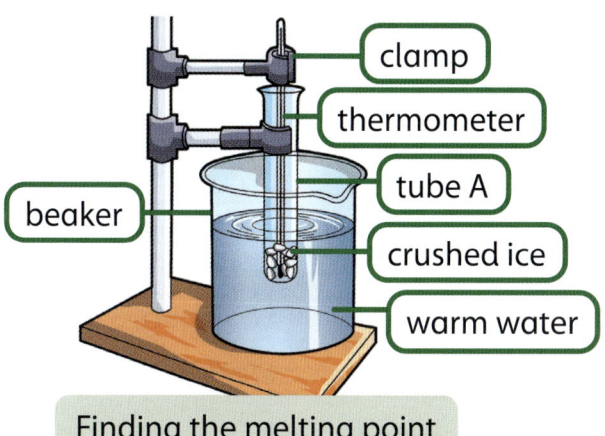
Finding the melting point

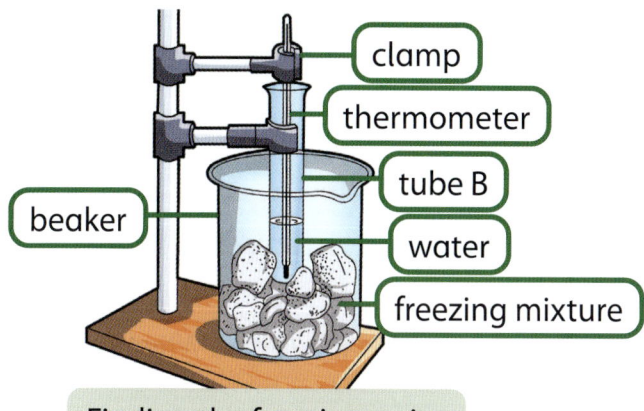
Finding the freezing point

At what temperature does water freeze and ice melt?

If you check in a book or on the internet, it will tell you that ice melts at 0°C. It will also tell you that water freezes at 0°C. We are going to find out if both of these statements are true.

1 Set up the apparatus and carry out the investigations.

2 Record your investigations.

3 With a partner, answer these questions in your notebook.

   a What makes the water in tube B cool down?

   b What makes the ice in tube A warm up?

   c At what temperature did the water freeze?

   d At what temperature did the ice melt?

   e Did you prove that water freezes at 0°C and ice melts at 0°C? Yes or no?

Be a scientist

Good scientists check the apparatus and read through all of the instructions before they start.

▶ pages 8–9

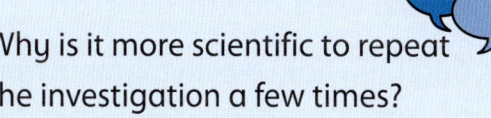

Why is it more scientific to repeat the investigation a few times?

Stretch zone

Use secondary sources to find out the melting points and freezing points for aluminium and candle wax. Compare your values with others in the class.

Key ideas

- The temperature when a solid changes to a liquid is known as its melting point. The temperature when a liquid changes to a solid is known as its freezing point.
- Materials have their own melting and freezing points.

1 Solids, Liquids and Gases

■ For more activities, go to Workbook 4 page 31.

Getting the water back

In this lesson you will learn that condensation is when a gas turns back into a liquid and is the reverse of evaporation.

Key words

condensation
evaporation

Think back

When water is heated, it changes to water vapour. What is this change of state called? If the water is heated to a higher temperature, it bubbles. What is very hot water vapour called?

Look at the photographs on this page. Discuss examples of when you have seen condensation.

You may have seen steam turning back into water on a cold surface.

A gas cooling and forming a liquid is called condensation. This is the opposite of evaporation.

Observing condensation

1 Carefully hold a cold mirror in front of your mouth. Breathe out gently.

   Record what you see.

2 Now pour cold water into a glass. Add ice cubes.

   Observe the sides of the glass. Record what you see.

3 Write a report that explains your observations.

   Include the words cold, water vapour, air and condensation in your report.

Stretch zone

Plan an investigation to find out if you can make condensation on a warm mirror. Predict your findings.

■ For more activities, go to Workbook 4 page 32.

Sometimes we need to slow down the process of evaporation. For example, we can cover plants with large plastic bags or sheets to stop them drying out.

Slowing down evaporation

You are going to write a plan of how to investigate different ways to slow down evaporation.

1 Think about doing the opposite of those things that speed up evaporation. Look back at page 27.

2 Think about how you will make it a fair test. Will you need to repeat measurements?

> How much water will you use?

> How many different methods will you try?

> How will you compare the different methods? What will you be measuring?

> How will you share your ideas and conclusions?

> How will you make your results reliable?

Key ideas

- The change in state of a gas to a liquid is called condensation. Cooling water vapour gives us liquid water.
- Condensation is the opposite of evaporation.

■ For more activities, go to Workbook 4 page 33.

The water cycle

In this lesson you will explore the changes of state in the water cycle.

Although 70% of the surface of the Earth is covered in water, only 5% of it is pure. The rest is mainly sea water and has dissolved salts and other substances in it. When sea water evaporates, the dissolved substances are left behind.

Why is it useful for living things on Earth that the water that evaporates from the seas and oceans is pure?

When it rains, water falls from clouds and on to the ground or into the sea.

The water on the ground can flow into rivers and then into lakes or the sea. The Sun then heats the water.

What would happen if all of the rain that falls stayed in the sea?

Air contains water vapour. If the air is cooled, the water vapour condenses. This water can fall as rain.

- Water can be heated by the Sun and move into the air as water vapour.

Look at the diagram. Discuss what is happening to the liquid water.

- Air can be cooled and the water vapour turns back to water.

As the water vapour cools, it forms clouds. When the clouds cool even more, the water will fall as rain or snow. This is called precipitation. This is how the Earth recycles water. This is called the water cycle.

■ For more activities, go to Workbook 4 page 34.

Study the diagram of the water cycle.

The water cycle

Remember that at higher temperatures, more evaporation occurs.

 Making an animated water cycle

You can make an animation using a flip book. Try to draw things moving only slightly on each page. Draw your pictures on the bottom half of each page.

1 Copy the sea, the Sun and the island from the diagram above onto the first page of your flip book.

2 On the next pages draw the Sun evaporating the sea.

3 On the next ones draw the clouds appearing.

4 On the later pages you can show clouds moving towards the island. They can then rise up for a few pages.

5 Finally, show water falling as rain and running into the sea.

Now flick the pages through your fingers and your animation will move.

Demonstrate your animation to others in your class.

Check how much you know.
Try the questions on pages 36–37.

Science fact

One billion tonnes of water falls to the Earth every minute. That's about 130 trillion kilograms of water!

Key idea

Condensation and evaporation are part of the water cycle and they recycle the water on Earth.

■ For more activities, go to Workbook 4 page 35.

1 Write the names of the three states of matter.

_____   _____   _____

2 Look at the following photographs of different materials.

a Tick the photographs that show solids.

b Underline the photographs that show liquids.

c Write down the name of one gas.

_____

3

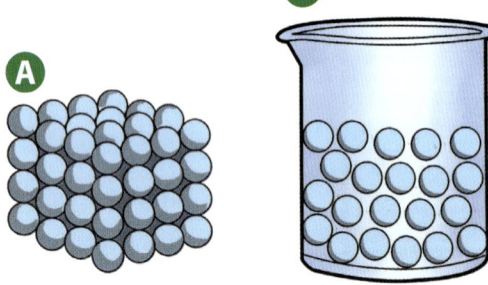

a Which of the diagrams above shows the particles in a solid?

b Which of the diagrams above shows the particles in a liquid?

c In the space below draw how the particles in a gas are arranged.

■ For more activities, go to Workbook 4 page 36.

4 Circle the correct word to finish each statement:

a Water dries up from a puddle by:

boiling   condensation   evaporation   freezing

b When a liquid is heated so much that bubbles form inside it, we call this:

boiling   condensation   evaporation   freezing

c Ice forms from water by:

boiling   condensation   evaporation   freezing

d Steam is made from water by:

boiling   condensation   evaporation   freezing

5 Write in the correct process for each stage of the water cycle. Use the words in the word box.

condensation   evaporation   precipitation

Sea water becomes water vapour in the air: _____

Water vapour becomes water in clouds: _____

Water in clouds falls as rain or snow: _____

6 Study the table below. Then answer the questions.

Material	Melting point (°C)	Boiling point (°C)
water	0	100
chocolate	30	180
iron	1535	2750
candle wax	65	360
diesel	−19	154

a Name one material in the table that is liquid at room temperature. _____

b Which material has the highest melting point? _____

c Is chocolate a solid or a liquid at 40°C? _____

■ For more activities, go to Workbook 4 page 37.

2 Habitats

In this unit you will:

- observe and group living things
- explore how different animals and plants live in different habitats
- use identification keys to identify living things
- find out how human activity can change environments and how this can put living things in danger.

Look closely at the map of the world and the photographs. The photographs show different animals living in different habitats.

What does the word 'habitat' mean?

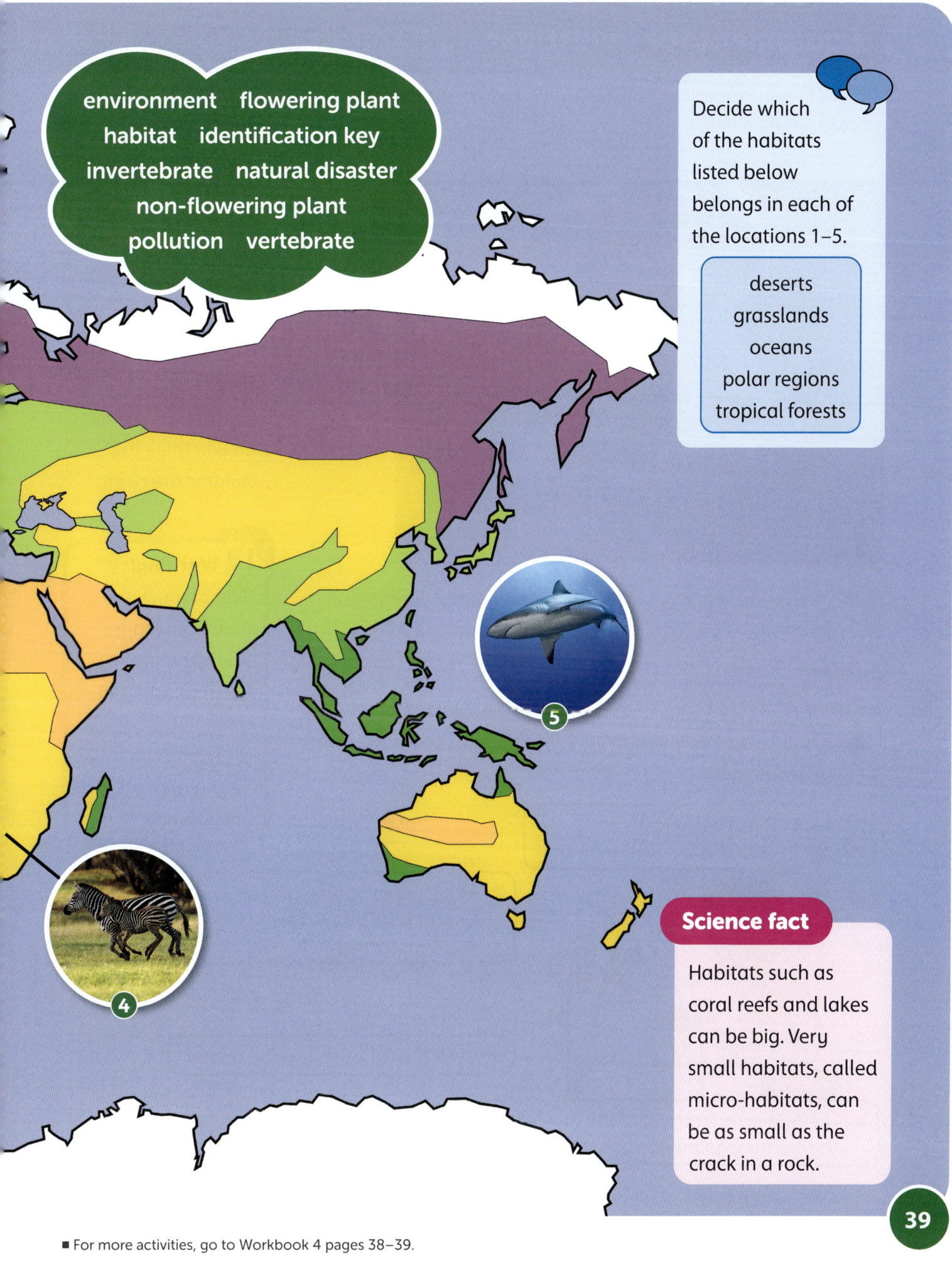

environment   flowering plant
habitat   identification key
invertebrate   natural disaster
non-flowering plant
pollution   vertebrate

Decide which of the habitats listed below belongs in each of the locations 1–5.

deserts
grasslands
oceans
polar regions
tropical forests

5

4

Science fact

Habitats such as coral reefs and lakes can be big. Very small habitats, called micro-habitats, can be as small as the crack in a rock.

■ For more activities, go to Workbook 4 pages 38–39.

Equipment for investigating habitats

In this lesson you will explore different ways to observe and classify livings things.

Key words

habitat
pooter
quadrat
sampling
sweep net

Look at the photograph. What do you think the children are doing?

Warning!
Do not touch the animals because they might sting. You must identify animals quickly and return them gently to their environment.

In this lesson we will look at the special equipment we can use to investigate what lives in different habitats.

Pooter

We use a pooter to capture small animals. We then use an identification key to identify them. It has pictures and names of different living things.

1 Place one end of the pooter tube in your mouth.

2 Place the other end of the pooter tube above the creature you want to capture.

3 Suck the creature into the pooter.

4 The netting on the end of the tube prevents the creature going into your mouth.

How to use a pooter

■ For more activities, go to Workbook 4 page 40.

Quadrat

We cannot count every single animal or plant in a habitat. Instead, we can use a quadrat or a trap to investigate a smaller area. This is called sampling the habitat.

Scientists sample different parts of a habitat to get a clue about the whole habitat.

1. Choose the place carefully. It needs to show a good example of what we can find in the habitat.

2. Place the quadrat gently on the ground. Or you could use a hoop.

3. Identify and count all the animals or plants you find inside the quadrat.

How to use a quadrat

Sweep net

We can use a sweep net in three ways to capture small animals.

Sweep the air

Sweep low-growing plants

Sweep a pond or stream

Pitfall trap

Pitfall traps are small cups set up beneath stones or leaves. Small animals fall into the traps and can be counted.

Decide which sweep net method to use for these examples:

a animals that live in water

b animals that live in plants

c flying animals.

Key idea

We can use special equipment to help us find living things in their natural habitat.

Stretch zone

Set up a pitfall trap and record the animals you find.

■ For more activities, go to Workbook 4 page 41.

2 Habitats

Investigating a local habitat

In this lesson you will plan and carry out an investigation about animals and plants in a local habitat.

Key words

environment
exoskeleton
hand lens
invertebrate/
vertebrate
pooter
quadrat

Think back

What is an invertebrate and what is a vertebrate? List three examples of each.

The goat has a hard skeleton inside its body. The crab has a hard skeleton outside its body. This is called an exoskeleton.

Animals with a backbone and an internal skeleton are called vertebrates. Those with no internal skeleton and no backbone are called invertebrates.

You are going to plan and conduct an investigation into plants and small animals in your local environment.

The environment is split up into many smaller habitats. A habitat is where animals and plants live and obtain what they need to survive.

> Classify the goat and crab as vertebrates or invertebrates.

> Talk about other animals you know that have an exoskeleton.

> What types of animals and plants will you look for?

Survey of local habitats

Your teacher will give you a map of the local habitats.

Decide where you will carry out your investigation. What will you look for when you get there?

> Look at the map. Discuss in your group the route you will take and the locations you will investigate.

1   Write your investigation plan. Include:

- title of investigation
- the methods you will use
- equipment
- safety rules
- locations
- predictions of what you will find.

■ For more activities, go to Workbook 4 page 42.

2 It is important to think about the best methods and equipment to use at each location.

- Sometimes you will use the pooter and the hand lens. Remember to count how many animals and plants you see.

- Sometimes you will use the quadrat or hoop. Count how many different animals and plants you find inside the quadrat or hoop, and count how many of each type.

3 Look carefully for plants and animals in cracks, and underneath stones or leaf piles.

Do not pick any wild flowers. Always return the animals to their habitat. If you see an animal you are unsure about, ask your teacher what it is.

Warning! Do not touch the animals and plants with your hands. Why do you think this is important?

4 Design a table to record all the animals and plants you find. An example is below.

Location	Equipment used	Animal	Plant	Number
footpath	quadrat	ants		50
footpath	hand lens	beetles		5

5 Design an information leaflet to tell people about the living things in your area.

Include how you found them and how many of each there were. Classify the animals as vertebrates or invertebrates.

Stretch zone

How do you think this location will change over a year? Write down some examples of the changes you would see and how they will affect the living things.

Key idea

We can plan investigations to find out about the living things in a habitat.

■ For more activities, go to Workbook 4 page 43.

Presenting data about local habitats

In this lesson you will explore ways to present data from your investigation about living things and habitats.

Key words
bar chart
data
habitat
interpret
pattern
table

Think back

How did you present the data you collected in your investigation into local habitats?

A results table is a very useful way of collecting data but is not always the best way to look for patterns or to present the data.

Interpreting data

The word 'data' means information. To interpret and understand data we need to ask the question: 'What is this data telling us?'

To help us answer this question, we can present the data in a bar chart. This makes the information easier to read and interpret.

Here is the table that one group used to record the number of animals they found.

Location	Animal	Number of animals
Site 1: footpath	ants	50
	caterpillars	0
	beetles	5
Site 2: playing field	ants	25
	caterpillars	1
	beetles	8
Site 3: flowerbed	ants	10
	caterpillars	30
	beetles	10

■ For more activities, go to Workbook 4 page 44.

They used their data to draw this bar chart.

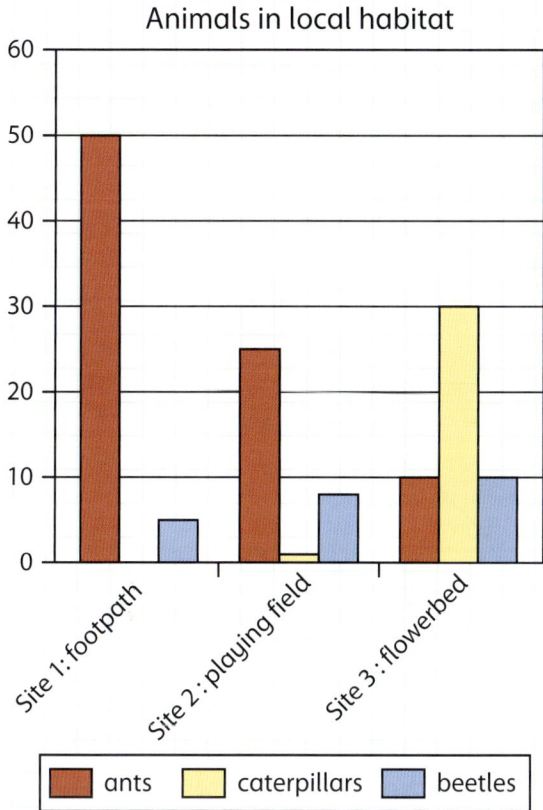

Animals in local habitat

Legend:
- ants
- caterpillars
- beetles

Study the bar chart. What is the data telling you about the animals? With a partner, answer these questions:

1 Which habitat do ants seem to prefer?

2 Which site had no caterpillars?

3 Which habitat did the caterpillars prefer?

4 Which sites contained examples of all of the animals?

Be a scientist

Scientists believe that placing a quadrat 16 times in an area will give the most reliable results. After 16 times, it is rare to find new animals.

Good scientists should always take a measurement more than once.

▶ page 9

Stretch zone

The ants may not have preferred the footpath. Think of a reason why a lot of ants were found there. What does this bar chart tell us?

Using data to make a bar chart

1 Use the data you collected with your group to create a bar chart.

2 Display your charts around the room.

3 Walk around to compare what the other groups found in their survey.

4 Use all of the graphs to work out:
- which animal was the most commonly seen
- which habitat had the most animals.

Key idea

Results tables are a useful way of recording data, but graphs and charts are often a better way to interpret and present patterns in the data.

2 Habitats

45

■ For more activities, go to Workbook 4 page 45.

Identification keys for animals

In this lesson you will learn how to use identification keys.

How can we find out the names of animals and plants we do not already know? We can use identification keys to help us.

Look at this example of an identification key.

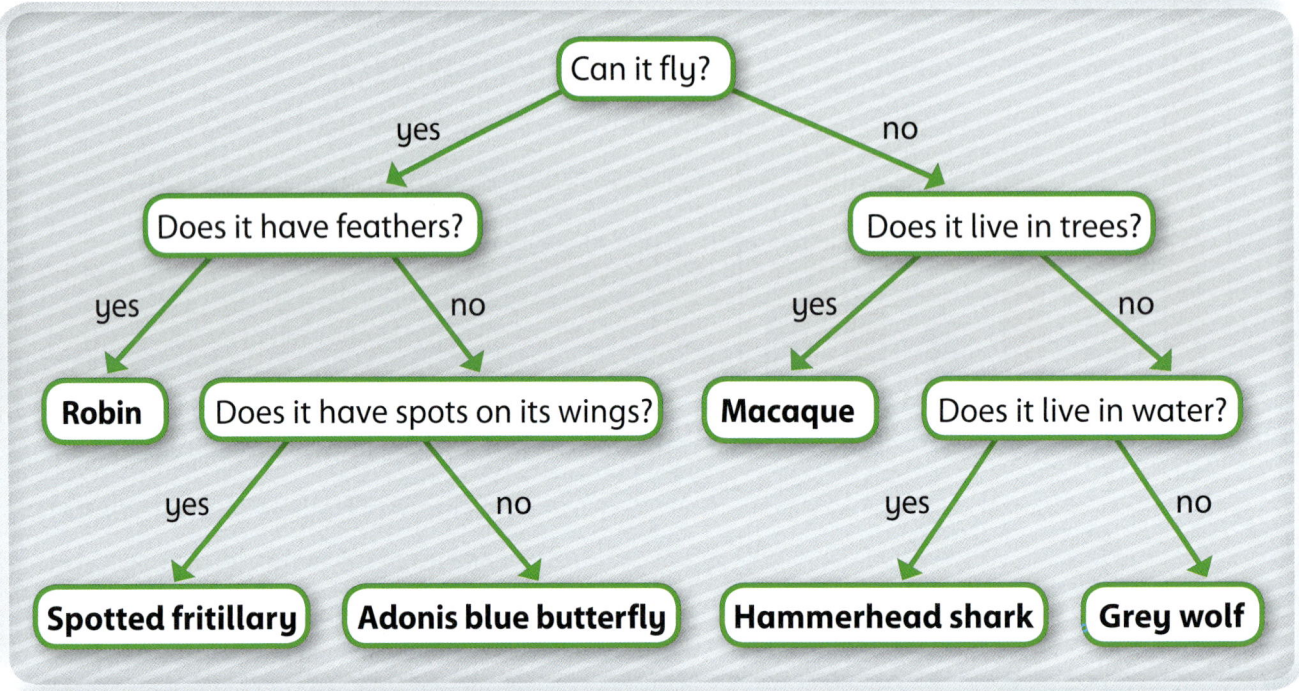

It is important that a key asks questions about what an animal or plant looks like. These are called the physical characteristics.

Discuss why the number of legs an animal has would be a better characteristic in a key than how tall it is.

Using a key

Use the identification key above to identify these animals.
Write their names in your notebook.

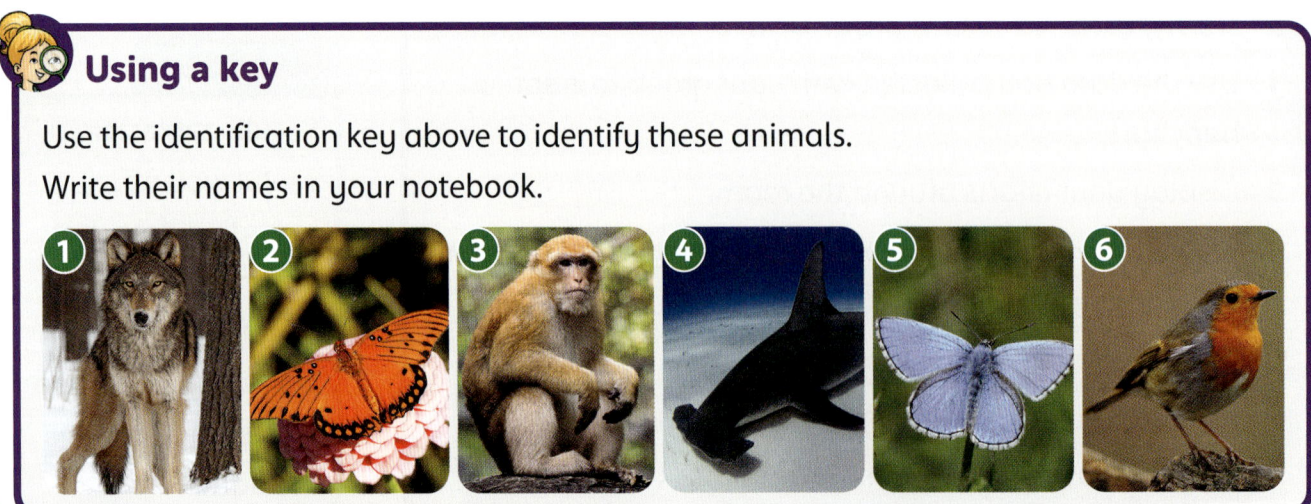

46

■ For more activities, go to Workbook 4 page 46.

Survey of vertebrates

Vertebrates can be grouped into five classes: mammals, birds, fish, reptiles and amphibians.

Your teacher will take you outside to survey some vertebrates.

1 Use the key to help you to decide which class of vertebrate each animal belongs to.

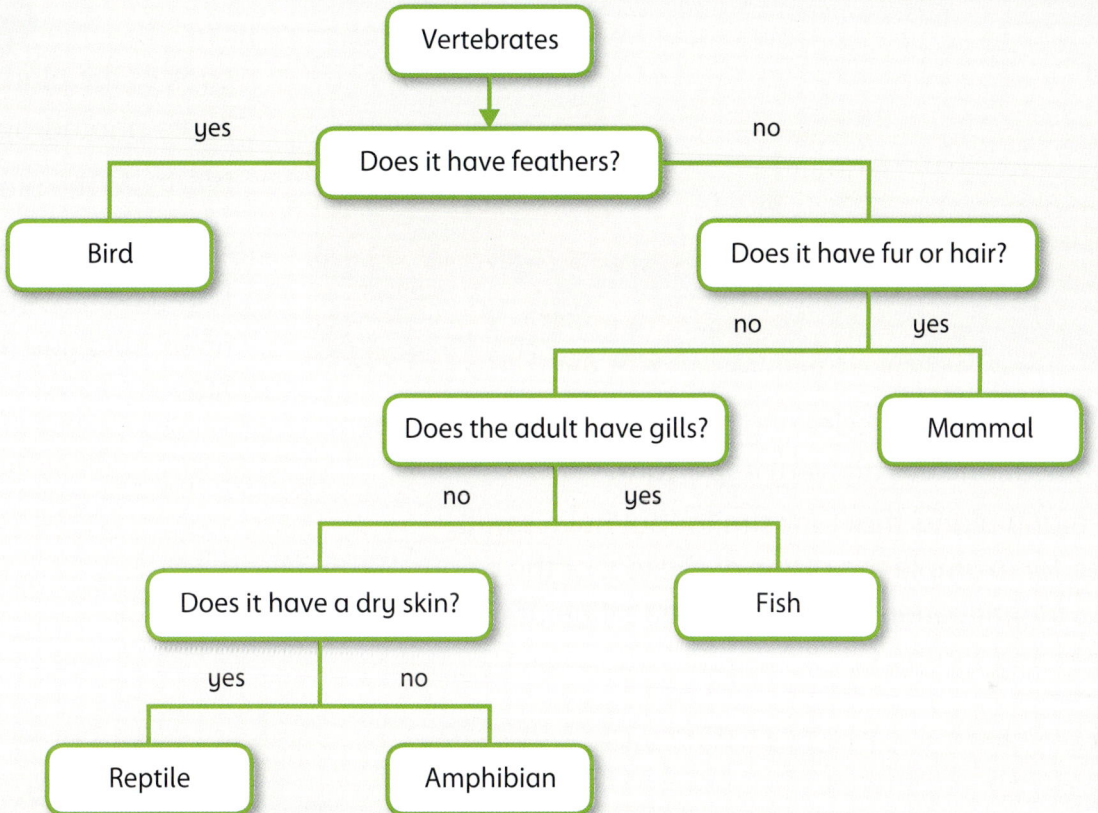

2 Record your observations in a table.

3 Use the data to find out which type of vertebrate was the most common.

How useful was the key?

4 Present your findings as a bar chart and compare it with others in your class.

Stretch zone

Search the internet to try to find a key for local birds. Identify any of the birds you saw in your survey in more detail.

Key idea

Scientists use keys to help them to identify living things they have never seen before.

■ For more activities, go to Workbook 4 page 47.

Identification keys for plants

In this lesson you will learn how to use identification keys for plants.

Key words

cactus
flowering plant/
non-flowering plant
identification key

Think back

Why do scientists use identification keys?

Look at the plants in the photograph.
What are the plants called?
If you do not know, how could you find out?

There are over 390 000 species of plants. No-one can know them all so identification keys are very important.

There are many plants that look similar but have small differences, for example the shape of the leaf or the colour of the flower. This identification key looks at two different types of plants: trees and shrubs.

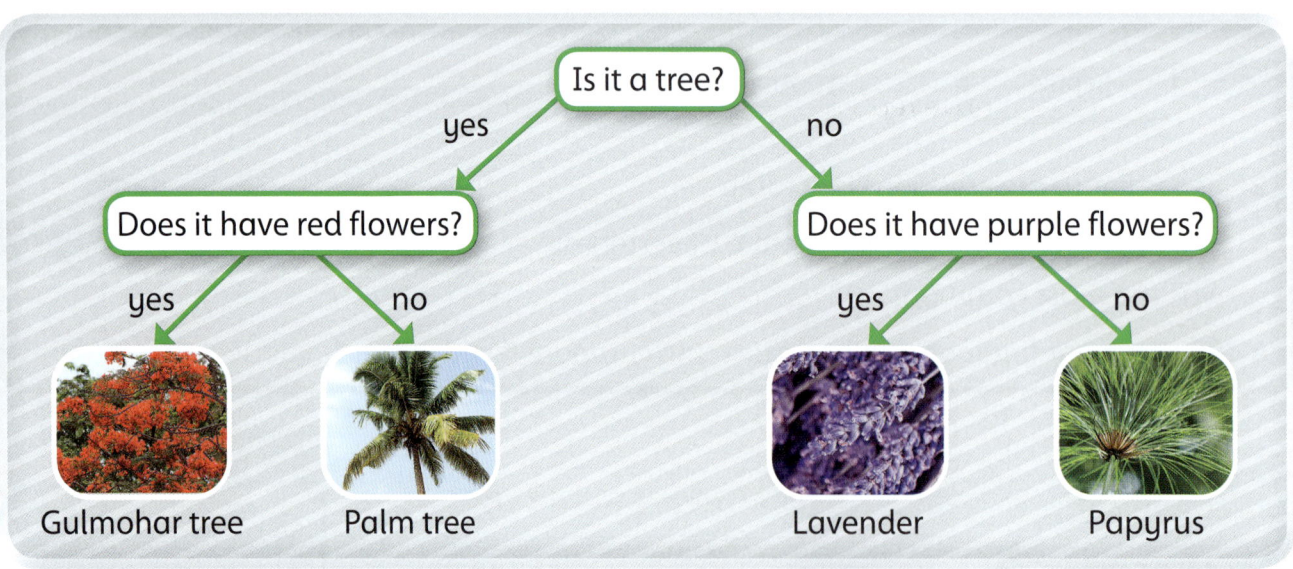

How did you decide if the plants are trees? Discuss the characteristics you used.

■ For more activities, go to Workbook 4 page 48.

People who sell flowers are known as florists. They have to know a lot about plants.

fern

moss

Ferns and mosses are non-flowering plants

Florist survey

You are going to survey the area where you live to find florists.

Your teacher may invite a florist to talk to your class.

1 Write some questions to find out how the florist knows about plants.

2 Find out how they learn to identify them. Do they use keys?

3 How many non-flowering plants do they use? How many flowering plants?

4 Write a thank-you letter to them after their visit. Include what you have learned about flowers from them.

Imagine your friend wants to buy a cactus with pink flowers. She thinks it is called a Saguaro. Use the key below to see if she is correct. If not, which cactus should she buy?

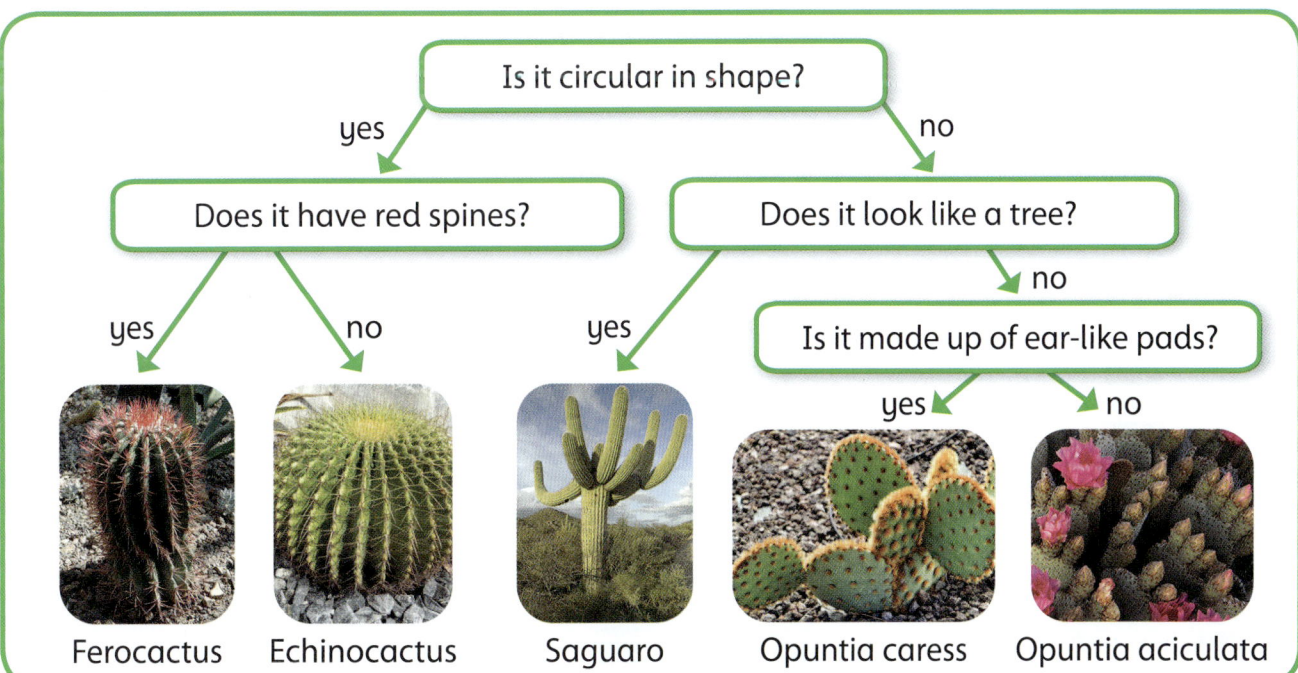

Is it circular in shape?
yes — Does it have red spines?
 yes — Ferocactus
 no — Echinocactus
no — Does it look like a tree?
 yes — Saguaro
 no — Is it made up of ear-like pads?
  yes — Opuntia caress
  no — Opuntia aciculata

Key idea

Identification keys can be used to help to identify plants.

■ For more activities, go to Workbook 4 page 49.

Fossil fuels

In this lesson you will find out how oil can affect the environment.

Key words
damage
environment
fossil fuel
non-renewable/
renewable
oil
pollution

Oil, coal and gas are know as fossil fuels. This is because they form from dead animals and plants that are buried deep in the ground. When these fuels are burned they cause air pollution.

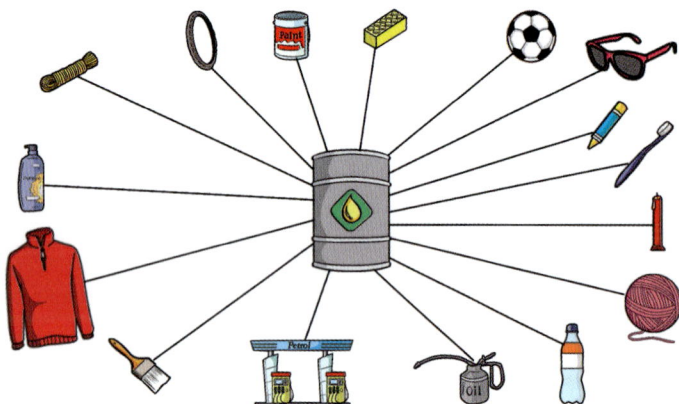

Oil can be used to make other materials such as plastics. These are very useful materials but they can cause pollution, especially in the oceans. Here they can trap and choke animals.

Oil takes millions of years to form naturally, deep within the Earth. This means it is a non-renewable material. Once it is used up it has gone forever.

Some energy sources, such as the wind, waves and solar power using the Sun, do not run out. These are called renewable.

This map shows the countries that have the most oil reserves.

Study the diagram showing the uses of oil.

Discuss some of the things that oil is used for.

Which of these have you used this week?

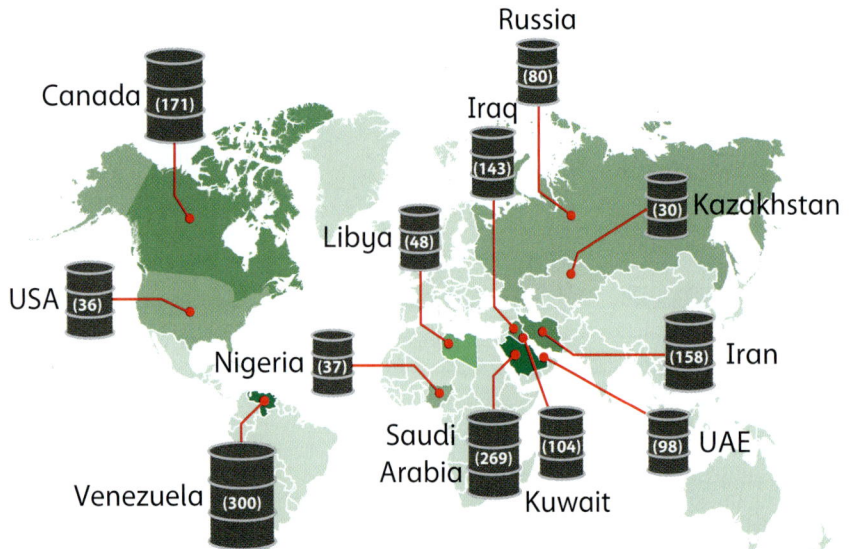

Russia (80)
Canada (171)
Iraq (143)
Kazakhstan (30)
Libya (48)
USA (36)
Nigeria (37)
Iran (158)
Saudi Arabia (269)
Kuwait (104)
UAE (98)
Venezuela (300)

The numbers show how many billions of barrels of oil each country has.

■ For more activities, go to Workbook 4 page 50.

Oil is taken from underground by drilling. It is sent to refineries to be made into useful products.

Sometimes oil can leak out into the environment. When humans add harmful materials to the environment it is called pollution.

Spilled oil can travel many kilometres across the oceans. It harms birds, fish and other animals that live in the sea. Everything gets covered in oil. When the oil slick reaches land, it pollutes the beaches and damages natural habitats.

Talk about the definition of pollution. How can we reduce the pollution caused by oil?

Researching oil spills

1 Use the internet or books to find out about an oil spill that has happened in your lifetime.

Find out where it was and how much oil was spilled. Describe the impact on living things.

How did people clean up the spill?

2 Make a short film or presentation about the spill to encourage people to be more aware of the dangers.

Key idea

Oil is a fossil fuel. It is a useful non-renewable resource, but it can cause damage to habitats.

Stretch zone

Research how coal is obtained. List some of the advantages and disadvantages of using coal in a table.

■ For more activities, go to Workbook 4 page 51.

2 Habitats

Air pollution

In this lesson you will investigate air pollution and how it affects the environment.

Key words
detector
pollution
renewable

Think back

Which use of oil is being shown in the photograph?

What is the evidence that the air in this city is polluted?

Discuss what you think is causing the pollution.

We all need air to breathe and to live. Animals also need air to breathe and to live. If there are high levels of air pollution, the air we breathe can cause harm to us and to other animals that breathe it.

Discuss all of the sources of air pollution shown here.

■ For more activities, go to Workbook 4 page 52.

We can measure air pollution. Some environmental scientists work in air pollution monitoring stations like the one shown in the photo. Monitoring stations collect data all day every day.

Making an air pollution detector

Solid particles in the air are one form of air pollution. You are going to make a detector for air pollution.

1 Take three paper plates. Rub a thin layer of petroleum jelly onto the surface of each plate. Any dirt in the air will settle onto the plates and make them dirty.

2 Leave two plates in different places outside to test air pollution. You will have to fix them so they do not blow away and protect them from getting wet.

3 Leave the third one inside the school where you think there might be some air pollution.

4 Check the plates every day for a week.

5 Which plate had the most air pollution? Why is this?

We can do lots of things to reduce air pollution. Here are some suggestions.

Polluter	Suggestion
factories	use clean energy from renewable sources
cars	walk or use public transport or hybrid cars
landfill sites	reduce waste
power stations	use clean energy from renewable sources

Stretch zone

Is there any air pollution where you live? Use the suggestions in the table to create a poster about reducing air pollution.

Key idea

Living things need air. Air pollution comes from many sources. It can be very harmful for living things.

2 Habitats

53

■ For more activities, go to Workbook 4 page 53.

River pollution

In this lesson you will investigate river pollution and how it affects the environment.

Rivers provide the habitats for many living things. Rivers come in many different shapes and sizes. Some rivers are wide and slow moving, others are narrow and fast flowing. Some rivers are very long, some rivers are very short.

Humans use rivers for many different reasons.

Let's look at how human activities can have an impact on a river and its surrounding habitats.

In the photograph opposite, we can see factories at the side of a river.

How do you think factories can have an impact on the river?

Key words
pollution
turbidity

Research the names of three rivers in your country.

Are these rivers clean or polluted?

Researching the human impact on rivers

These photographs show human activities on or near to a river.

1 Use the information in the photographs to help you to think about the problems humans can cause to rivers.

2 Use the internet to find out some of the ways rivers can be protected. Make an information leaflet to share your ideas.

■ For more activities, go to Workbook 4 page 54.

The polluted water is very dirty and difficult to see through

Investigating river water

You are going to test river water samples to see which have the most pollution in them. To do this you are going to use a disk called a turbidity disk. Turbidity means cloudiness.

1 Draw your own disk like the one in the picture.

1 2 3 4 5 6 7 8 9 10

2 Place each sample onto the disk. Look through the sample and note which lines you can see. Record the number of the lightest line you can see.

3 Which river water sample was the cleanest? Which was the most polluted?

Stretch zone

The oceans of the world are polluted. Research some of the ways that pollution enters the oceans and present your ideas about how this could be prevented.

■ For more activities, go to Workbook 4 page 55.

Science fact

Water is special. It expands when it is heated and it is able to dissolve many materials. It has such small particles it should be a gas but the particles are held together. So, luckily for living things, it is a liquid between 0 and 100°C.

Key ideas

- Human activities affect rivers in many ways.
- Rivers are very important to living things and should be protected from damage.

Natural disasters – tsunamis

In this lesson you will find out how tsunamis can affect the environment.

Key words

natural disaster

tsunami

wave

What is a tsunami?

A tsunami is a natural event. We cannot prevent tsunamis but we can prepare for them.

A tsunami is formed when there are movements of the Earth's surface under the oceans. These movements include underwater volcanic eruptions, landslides and earthquakes. These movements create waves that move in all directions.

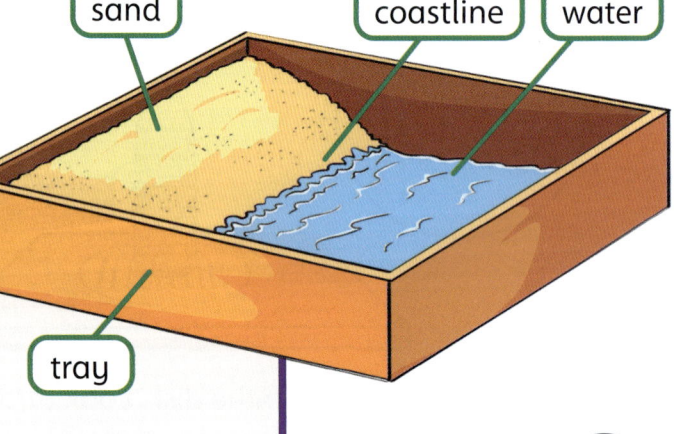

sand   coastline   water

tray

Investigating waves

1. Set up a sand tray as in the diagram. You can add model houses and twigs for trees.

2. Use a small piece of wood to help you to make waves. Start by moving the wood backwards and forwards slowly.

3. Observe what happens to the coastline. Film it if you can.

4. Next, move the wood backwards and forwards quickly to make large waves.

5. Observe what happens to the coastline. Film it if you can.

6. Use your sand tray to investigate ways to protect the coastline from giant waves or tsunamis.

What did your investigation tell you about how waves damage a coastline?

Discuss two ways that people can protect the coastline.

■ For more activities, go to Workbook 4 page 56.

Preparing for tsunamis

We have seen how tsunamis are formed, but what can we do about them?

Many people can be hurt or killed when large tsunamis hit coastal areas. Large tsunamis can also cause a lot of damage to the environment.

TSUNAMI HAZARD ZONE

In case of earthquake IMMEDIATELY go to higher ground or move inland

A sign is a way of warning people

 Be a scientist

Scientists share and discuss ideas so they can develop the most useful plans and processes.

▶ page 8

How can we protect habitats from the effects of tsunamis?

 How can we prepare for tsunamis?

1 Use these suggestions to write an action plan for how a community can prepare for tsunamis.

- Move away from the coast quickly.
- Have an early warning system in places where tsunamis are likely to occur.
- Arrange where you will meet your family and friends if you are separated from them.
- Make your way quickly to higher ground.
- Make sure you know how to contact your family if there is a tsunami warning.
- Make sure you follow any instructions given.

2 Compare your action plan with others in your group. Did you all have the same actions?

3 Work as a team to agree on the final actions to be included in your plan.

Key idea

Tsunamis are natural and can cause a lot of damage to the environment and the habitats in it.

■ For more activities, go to Workbook 4 page 57.

Natural disasters – volcanoes

In this lesson you will find out how volcanoes affect the environment.

Key words
eruption
volcano

This photograph shows the volcano Mauna Loa in Hawaii. It is the biggest volcano in the world.

What is happening in the photograph? What damage is being caused to habitats?

Volcanoes are one of the most dramatic natural things in our world. There are three classes of volcanoes: active; dormant; extinct.

What is a volcano?

A volcano is an opening in the Earth's crust. Let's look inside a volcano.

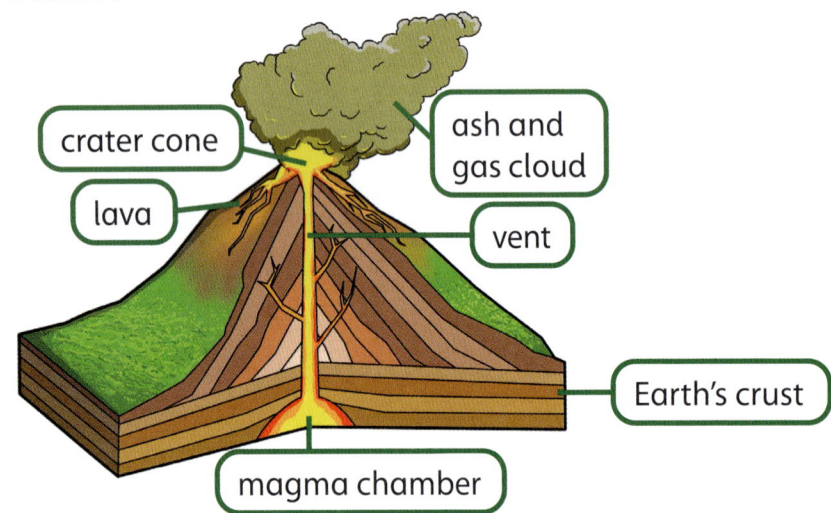

crater cone

lava

ash and gas cloud

vent

Earth's crust

magma chamber

Science fact

Ash and gases released from volcanic eruptions can reach heights of over 30 kilometres above the surface of the Earth!

The magma chamber is where an eruption starts.

Magma is very hot liquid rock. When pressure in the magma chamber builds up too high, it needs to escape. This is when eruptions happen.

The magma is forced up the vent very quickly and erupts from the crater. When the magma leaves the volcano it is called lava. The erupting volcano also releases ash and gas clouds.

■ For more activities, go to Workbook 4 page 58.

Making a volcano

You will need some modelling clay, a small container, a large tray, washing-up liquid, water, two tablespoons of baking soda, some vinegar with red food colouring in it.

1 Place your container in the middle of the tray. Use the modelling clay to create the shape of a volcano. Leave the top of the volcano open for the eruption.

2 Put the baking soda inside the container in your volcano.

 Add a little warm water and a few drops of washing-up liquid.

3 Pour the red vinegar into the container. Observe what happens.

Warning!

Be careful with vinegar. Wear eye protection and wash off any spills with water.

What could happen if you did not do this?

Discuss with a partner how your volcano models the eruption of a real volcano.

How do human activities affect volcanic regions?

Many tourists find volcanoes fascinating because of the unusual landscape features.

Can you think of any problems that large-scale tourism creates in volcanic regions?

Key idea

The lava, gases and ash produced by a volcano can cause a great deal of damage to the environment and the habitats in it.

Stretch zone

Research some advantages that volcanoes can bring to areas in the longer term. Write a short report.

■ For more activities, go to Workbook 4 page 59.

2 Habitats

Natural disasters – earthquakes

In this lesson you will discover how earthquakes can affect the environment.

Look at this diagram of a model seismograph. What do you think it measures?

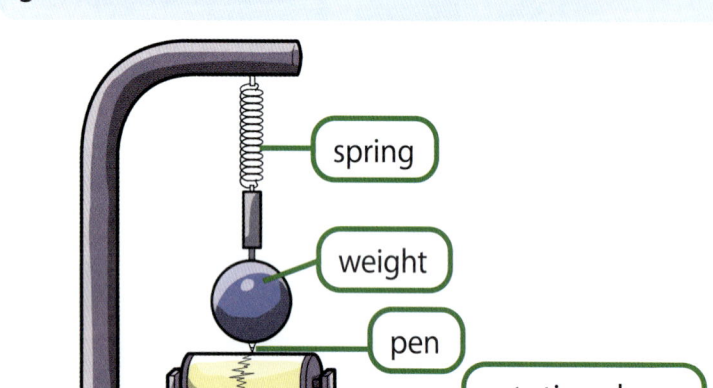

spring

weight

pen

rotating drum

← horizontal motion →

Earthquakes are natural disasters and we cannot stop them from happening.

Imagine that the Earth's crust is like a huge jigsaw with pieces that do not quite fit together, like in the map below. The scientific name for these jigsaw pieces is tectonic plates. Sometimes the tectonic plates move and cause earthquakes.

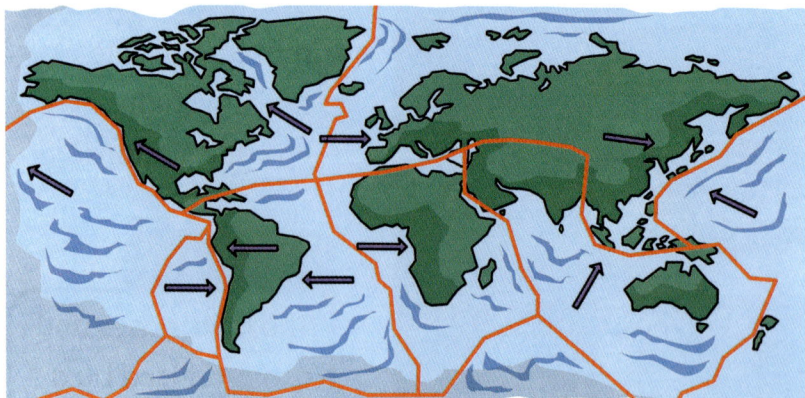

Scientists use seismographs to measure the movement of the Earth. They can give early warnings when there is going to be an earthquake.

The strength, or magnitude, of an earthquake is measured using the Richter scale of 0–10.

Science fact

The biggest earthquake recorded was in 1960 in Chile. It had a magnitude of 9.5 and led to a tsunami 25 metres high. A lot of people died.

■ For more activities, go to Workbook 4 page 60.

Earthquakes can destroy buildings, and people can be trapped under the fallen buildings. Fires often start.

We can prepare for earthquakes. We can design buildings that are earthquake-proof.

Burj Khalifa, Dubai

Transamerican Pyramid, San Francisco

What do you notice about these buildings?

 Designing an earthquake-proof building

You will work with a team to design and make an earthquake-proof building.

1 Use dry spaghetti as your building material. Hold your building together with glue or very small pieces of sticky tape.

2 Test your building by placing a 100 g weight onto the top and shaking the table backwards and forwards.

Did your building survive the earthquake?

3 Which designs were the best at surviving the shaking?

 Be a scientist

Scientists study their results and think about how well their investigation worked. Then they improve it. This is called evaluation.

▶ page 13

 Stretch zone

Are there any earthquake-proof buildings in your city or country? What do they all have in common?

Check how much you know.
Try the questions on pages 62–63.

Key idea

Earthquakes can cause a lot of damage to buildings and the environment and the habitats in them.

2 Habitats

61

■ For more activities, go to Workbook 4 page 61.

What have I learned about habitats?

1 Name these pieces of equipment used to investigate habitats.

_____   _____   _____   _____

2 Tick the photographs that show a non-flowering plant. There is more than one answer.

3 **a** Write down two environmental problems caused by volcanoes.

_____   _____

b Write down two environmental advantages of volcanoes.

_____   _____

4

Write down two ways that coastlines can be protected from storms and tsunamis.

■ For more activities, go to Workbook 4 page 62.

_____   _____

5 Use the key to identify the two animals. Write the name of each one on the answer line.

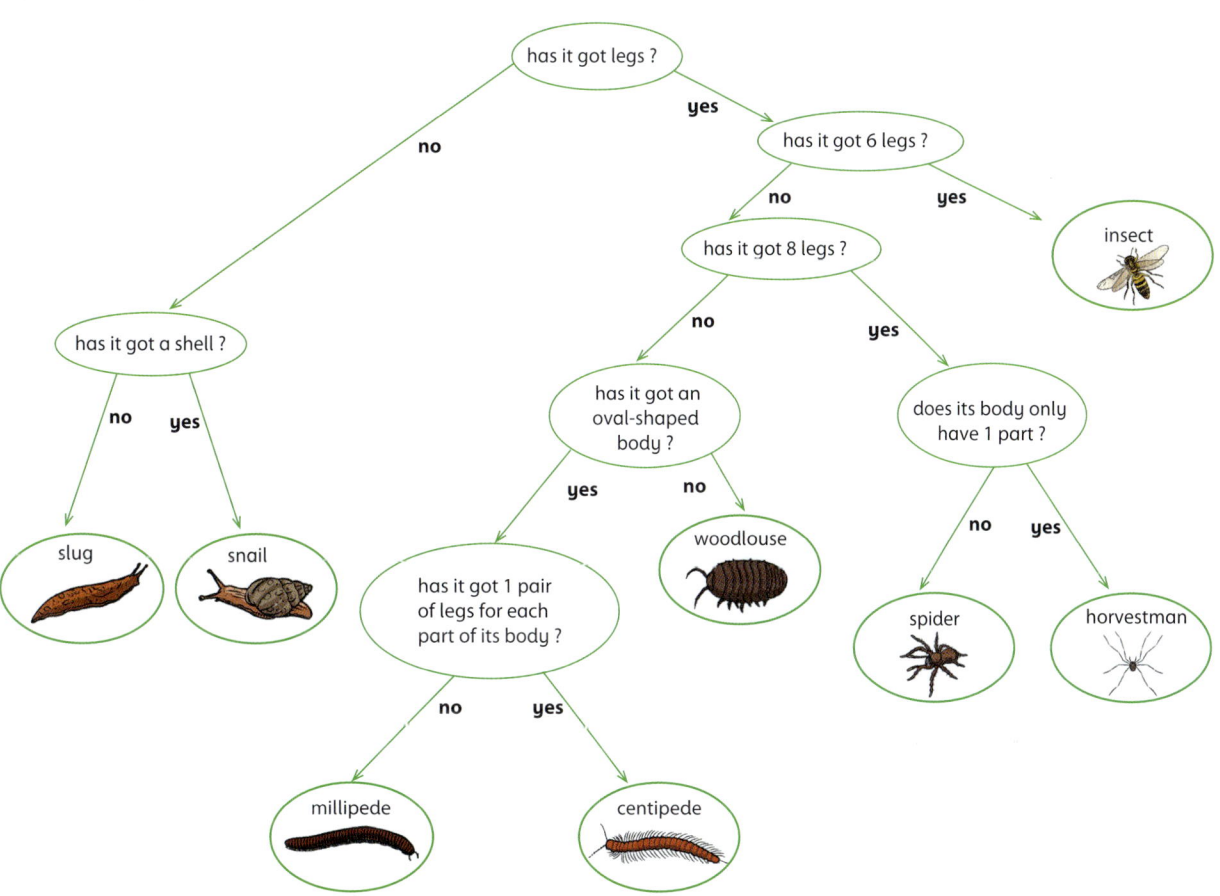

_____   _____

6 Study the table below. It shows the number of animals collected in three pitfall traps.

Location	Number of ants	Number of woodlice	Number of slugs
sunny, dry place	15	0	1
damp, dark place	0	2	12
dry, dark place	4	16	4

a Which animal prefers sunny, dry places? _____

b Which animal prefers dry, dark places? _____

c Which animal prefers damp, dark places? _____

d Explain why slugs avoid sunny, dry places. _____

■ For more activities, go to Workbook 4 page 63.

In this unit you will:

- explore the digestive system in humans
- identify types of teeth and their functions
- explore how the sense of taste can guide us to eat the right foods
- find out how food chains can be used to show feeding relationships
- explore and construct food chains for different habitats
- learn about the words 'producer', 'consumer', 'predator' and 'prey'.

Look carefully at these skulls. How are the teeth different?

Why are the cheetahs chasing the antelope?

Are these animals carnivores, herbivores or omnivores?

carnivore   consumer
digestive system   food chain
herbivore   omnivore
predator   prey   producer
taste   teeth

Science fact

Blue whales grow to over 25 metres in length yet they eat tiny shrimp-like creatures called krill.

■ For more activities, go to Workbook 4 pages 64–65.

Breaking down food

In this lesson you will learn how food is broken down in the human digestive system.

Think back

Which nutrients have you heard of? Make a list.

Key words

digestion

digestive system

energy

enzyme

nutrient

Nutrients are essential for life. We get nutrients by eating and drinking.

The nutrients in food give us energy and the materials for our bodies to grow and stay healthy. They must be broken down into smaller parts to pass into our bodies.

This is called digestion.

You will learn more about food types later in this unit.

Testing foods to see if they contain energy

You are going to burn some food samples to see which ones have the most energy.

 Warning! You must wear eye protection and do not touch anything that is hot.

1 Fix one of the samples of food to the end of the needle.

2 Hold it in a candle flame and observe what happens.

3 Record your observations in a table.

4 Repeat this for all the different types of food.

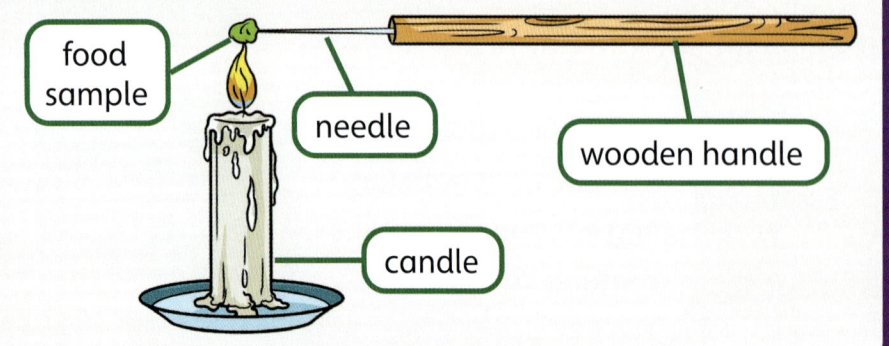

food sample

needle

wooden handle

candle

Be a scientist

Scientists record results as soon as they finish their observations so they do not forget any details.

▶ page 11

What does your investigation tell you about how much energy each food contained?

■ For more activities, go to Workbook 4 page 66.

During digestion, foods are broken down step-by-step. This happens as the food passes through the digestive system. The breakdown of food is helped by chemicals called enzymes. Each enzyme breaks down a particular food.

Digestion starts in the **mouth**. Food is chewed and mixed into a paste. A liquid called saliva helps to soften the food.

The paste is swallowed and passes down the **oesophagus** to the stomach.

Bile from the **liver** enters the small intestine and helps to break down fats and oils.

Enzymes are also added from the **pancreas** in the small intestine. These break down other fats and also proteins and sugars.

In the **stomach**, the food paste is mixed with acids and enzymes. From the stomach, the paste travels to the small intestine.

In the **large intestine**, water enters the body. Waste food then passes out of the body into the toilet.

Most food enters the body through the **small intestine**.

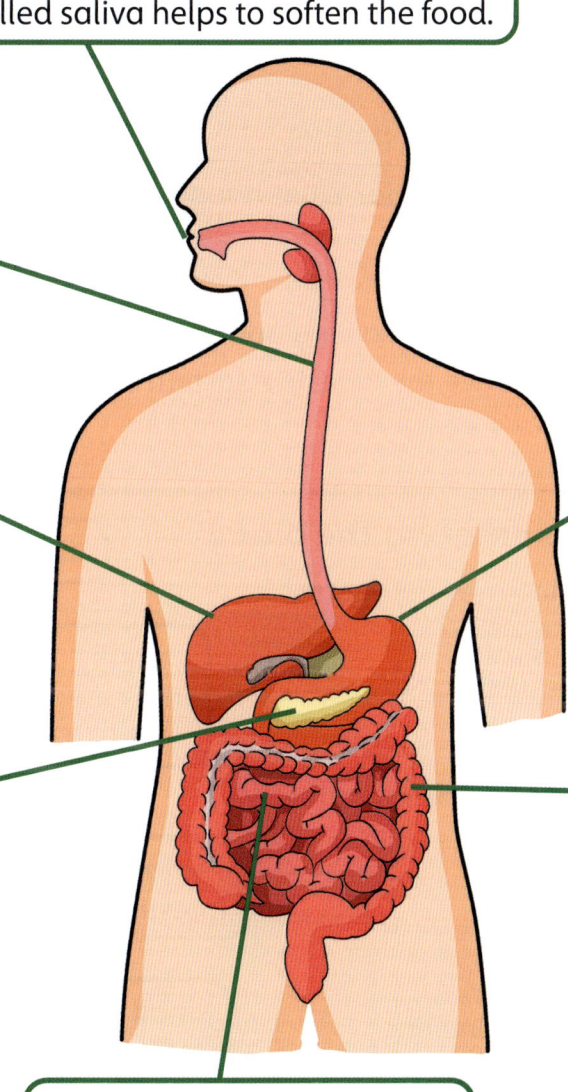

Key idea

Nutrients are broken down step-by-step in the digestive system by chewing, mixing and enzymes. They become smaller parts that can enter the body.

■ For more activities, go to Workbook 4 page 67.

3 Digestion and Food Chains

Absorbing nutrients

In this lesson you will find out how nutrients are taken into the body from the digestive system.

Key words
absorption
blood
surface

Think back

How many parts of the digestive system can you remember?

Discuss the functions of the mouth, stomach and liver.

Science fact

The walls of the small intestine are lined with tiny fingers and folds. This makes more surfaces for nutrients to pass through.

Discuss the following questions with a partner.

What are enzymes and what do they do? What happens in the small intestine?

The small intestine is a narrow tube with a very good blood supply. It is here that nutrients leave the digestive system and enter the blood.

Modelling nutrients entering the blood

Look at the diagram showing how nutrients enter the blood.

You are going to make a model or a poster to show how this happens.

You can use small cards to add labels to your model or poster.

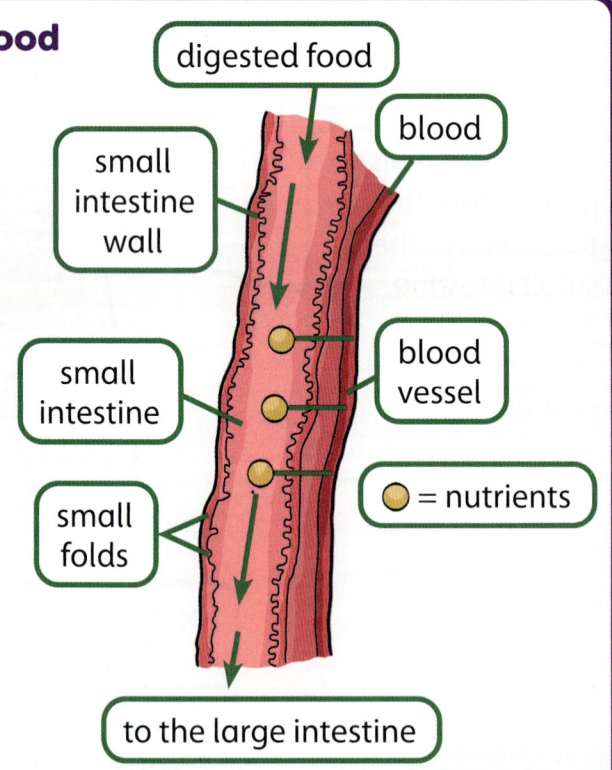

digested food

blood

small intestine wall

blood vessel

small intestine

= nutrients

small folds

to the large intestine

Stretch zone

Research how the small intestine has adapted to carry out its job. Add information to your model or poster to share your findings.

How is the small intestine adapted to help it do its job?

Why does it need a good blood supply?

■ For more activities, go to Workbook 4 page 68.

Remember that in the digestive system food is broken down into smaller nutrients. This is done by chewing, churning and mixing. It is also helped by chemicals, such as enzymes and acids.

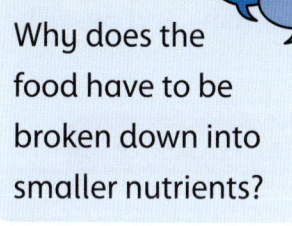

Why does the food have to be broken down into smaller nutrients?

Making a digestive system display

You are going to design and make a digestive system display in a group.

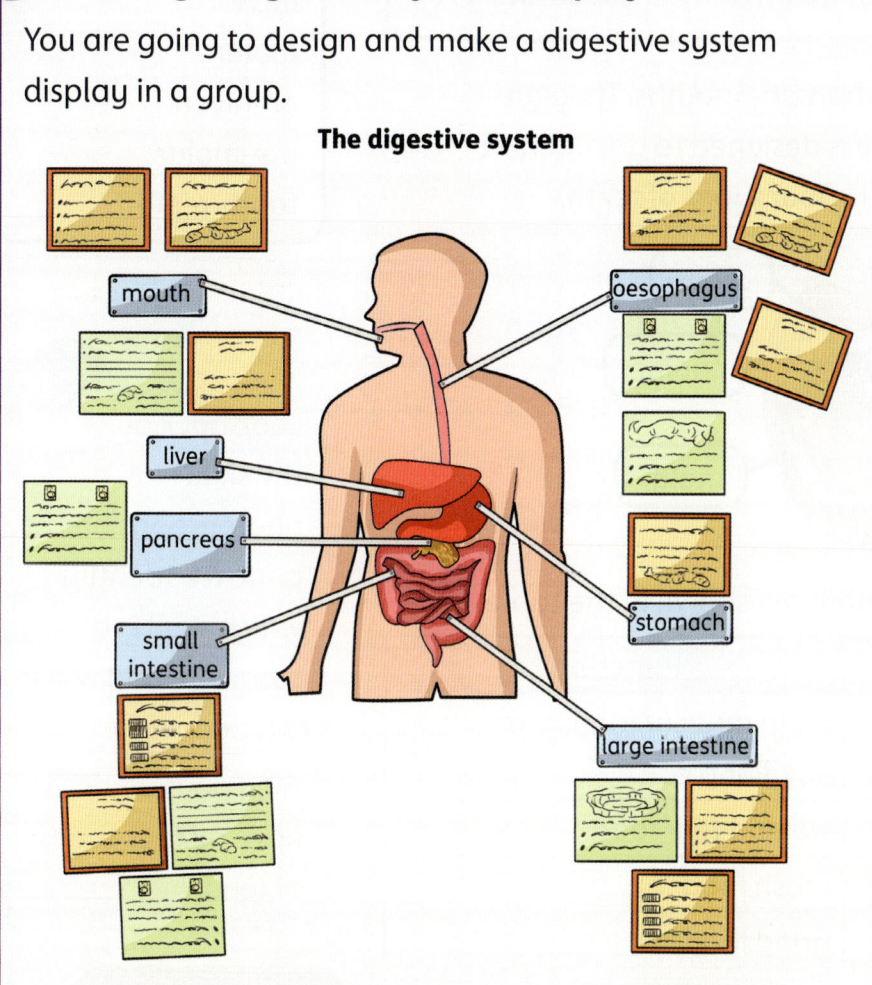

The digestive system

mouth

oesophagus

liver

pancreas

small intestine

stomach

large intestine

Be a scientist

Scientists use poster displays to share their work and conclusions with other scientists.

▶ page 13

1. Make your poster bright, clear and colourful.
2. Include a model of the digestive system and label it.
3. Add information and facts.
4. Create a classroom exhibition and walk around to learn from other displays.

Stretch zone

Research what fibre is. Write down why it is important in human digestion and health.

Key ideas

- Nutrients are absorbed through the walls of the small intestine into the blood.
- Water is absorbed into the body from the large intestine.

3 Digestion and Food Chains

69

■ For more activities, go to Workbook 4 page 69.

Teeth

In this lesson you will identify the different types of teeth in humans and describe their functions.

Think back

What happens to food in your mouth as you are eating it?

There are four types of teeth in humans mouths. They are surrounded by gums. Each type is designed to do different things. Humans have a mix of the four types of teeth.

Key words
canine
carnivore
herbivore
incisor
molar
omnivore
pre-molar
tooth/teeth

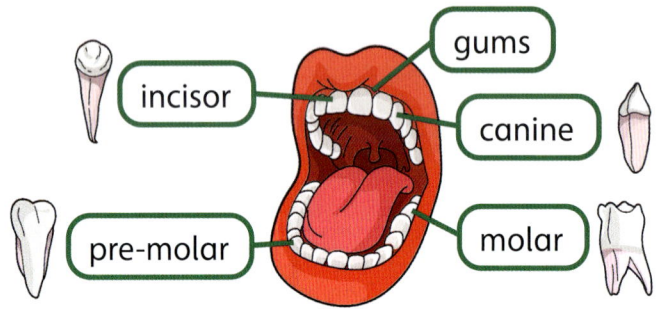

The functions of each type of tooth are shown in the table.

Type of tooth	Function
incisors	chop and cut food into smaller pieces
canines	rip and tear food
pre-molars	crush food
molars	grind food

Carnivores have long canine teeth to help them to tear meat up.

Look back at the skull photographs on page 64. Identify which skull is a carnivore and which is a herbivore.

Why does a human have all four types of teeth?

Science fact

Teeth are covered with a material called enamel. This is the hardest material in the body but it can still be damaged.

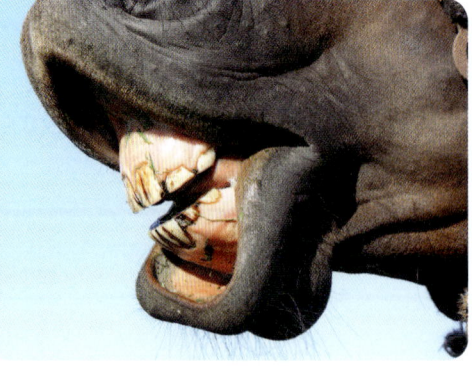

Herbivores have small canine teeth but large pre-molars and molars to crush and grind grass, leaves and seeds.

■ For more activities, go to Workbook 4 page 70.

 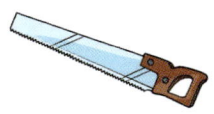  

Which tool would you choose to cut the wood into three pieces? Why would you not use the other tools?

Just like tools, your teeth are designed to carry out different jobs.

Modelling teeth

Your teacher will give you some tools and objects. Try to use the different tools to help you to break the objects you have been given into small pieces. The objects represent different foods. The tools represent different types of teeth.

Warning! You will be using sharp tools. Never point them towards you or someone else. Never move around with them. Discuss why this is important.

1 Use each tool on each object.

2 Record your observations.

3 Decide which tool represents each type of tooth.

4 Share your ideas by designing a poster display of your findings.

Discuss why it is important to look after your teeth.

Teeth are very important for digestion. They break down the large pieces of food into smaller pieces. This makes it easier to swallow them.

In the mouth the chewing action also helps the food to be mixed with saliva. This is a liquid that helps the food to change into a paste. The smooth paste is easier to swallow than dry food. The saliva also contains an enzyme that starts to break down starchy foods such as bread, rice and pasta.

 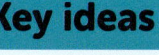 **Stretch zone**

Research the sabre-toothed tiger. Explain how fossils show that this animal was a carnivore. Download or draw some pictures.

Key ideas

- Humans have four different types of teeth to do different jobs.
- Animal teeth are adapted to what the animal eats.

3 Digestion and Food Chains

■ For more activities, go to Workbook 4 page 71.

Taste

In this lesson you will explore our sense of taste.

Key words
sense
taste
taste bud
tongue

Do you like sweet things or sour things?

What is your favourite taste?

We need to eat lots of different kinds of food to stay healthy. These foods have many different flavours.

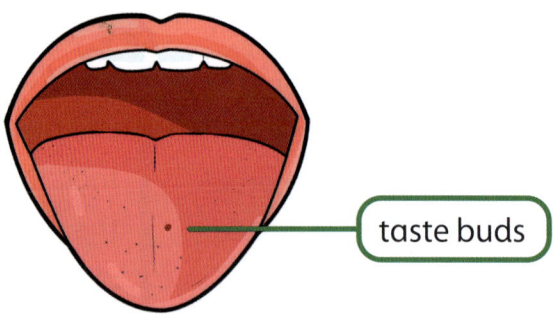

taste buds

The tongue is covered in tiny taste buds that help us to taste. You can use a mirror and a magnifying glass to help you see the taste buds on your tongue.

All the foods you can think of are in the four taste groups:

| sweet | bitter | sour | salty |

Some foods have a mixture of different tastes. Some scientists include savoury food as a fifth group.

Science fact

We have about 10 000 taste buds in our mouth and, in general, girls have more than boys!

■ For more activities, go to Workbook 4 page 72.

Which parts of the tongue have the most taste buds?

You are going to find out which parts of your tongue have the most taste buds.

1 Put a lolly stick in a cup of flavoured water.

2 Place it on different parts of your tongue:

- the front
- the sides
- the top
- under your tongue.

3 Which parts of your tongue tasted the flavour the most?

4 Draw a picture of a tongue like these. Colour the tongue to show where you tasted the flavour most.

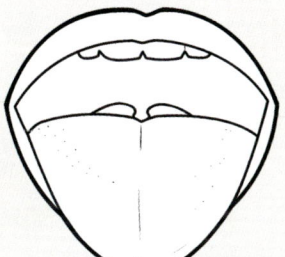 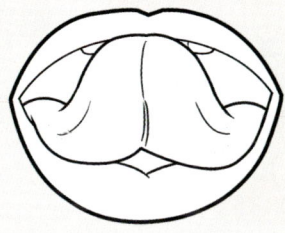

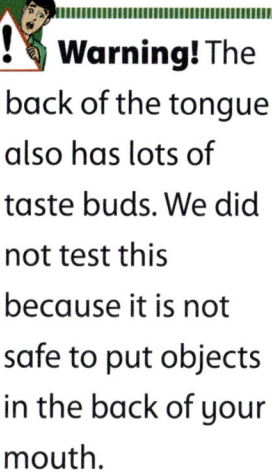

Warning! The back of the tongue also has lots of taste buds. We did not test this because it is not safe to put objects in the back of your mouth.

Compare your tongue map with your group. Does it look the same or does it look different?

Taste survey

There are sweet, salty, sour, bitter and savoury foods. Which foods are most popular?

1 Carry out a survey of your class. Find out which is the most popular taste. Copy and complete the table using tally marks.

Taste	Number of students
bitter	
salty	
savoury	
sour	
sweet	

2 Show the results you recorded in the table as a bar chart.

Key idea

We use our tongues to taste things.

■ For more activities, go to Workbook 4 page 73.

Sorting foods into groups

In this lesson you will explore how taste can guide us to eat the right types of food.

Key words

carbohydrate

fat

fibre

protein

salt

vitamin

Think back

Can you remember the five taste groups?

Many of the foods we eat taste good. There are lots of different foods. Our body tells us when we are short of foods when we feel hungry. Taste helps our body to decide which things are safe to eat.

Sweet foods give us energy. Sweet foods contain different food groups, including carbohydrates.

Savoury foods often contain protein. Protein helps us grow.

We need some salt in our bodies to keep us healthy. It is important not to have too much salt.

Sour and bitter foods often contain vitamins, which keep us healthy.

Foods that cannot be digested are called fibre. Fibre helps food to pass through the digestive system.

Look at the examples of foods in the photographs. Talk about which of these foods you eat the most. What do the foods give to your body to help it to stay healthy and grow?

We also need water in our diet. We get this from drinking and from foods that contain water.

■ For more activities, go to Workbook 4 page 74.

Scientists split foods into different groups. Examples are shown in the table.

Food group	Examples of foods
proteins	meats, eggs, nuts, beans, cheese, milk
carbohydrates	bread, pasta, potatoes, sweet fruits, honey
fats and oils	meat, milk, vegetable oils, avocado, cheese
vitamins and minerals	fruits, vegetables, eggs, cheese, fish

Sorting food into groups

1 Your teacher will give you some different foods. Work with a partner to sort the foods into the different food groups in the table.

Warning! Some people react badly to some foods. This is an allergy. Tell your teacher if you have any allergies to foods such as peanuts.

Proteins	Carbohydrates	Fats and oils	Vitamins and minerals

2 Keep a food diary of all the foods you eat in a day. Sort the foods into protein, fat, fruit, vegetables or any other food groups that you have eaten.

3 Find pictures in magazines and catalogues of the food you have eaten. Cut the pictures out and stick them into the food groups. This can be a visual version of your food diary. Don't forget to cut out more pictures of the same food if you ate it more than once.

Which food group did you eat from the most?

Stretch zone

Research how the sense of taste protects us. Present your examples to the class.

Key idea

Taste tells us which foods we need to eat to stay healthy and which foods to avoid.

■ For more activities, go to Workbook 4 page 75.

Unhealthy foods

In this lesson you will learn that some foods can be unhealthy.

Key words

diabetes

heart disease

obesity

Think back

Why is the heart so important?

What would happen if it wasn't healthy?

Look at the lunch box. Which of the foods do you think are healthy and which are unhealthy?

A blocked artery supplying blood to the heart.

We need to eat some fatty foods to keep us warm and to give us energy, but we cannot eat too many because this will harm our bodies.

If we eat too many fatty foods, it can damage our health.

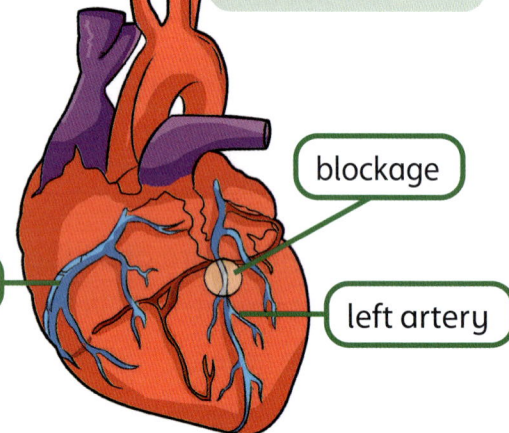

blockage

right artery

left artery

Stretch zone

Research how fatty foods can damage the heart and blood vessels. Write down your ideas.

If someone eats too much sugar and does not exercise, it can be difficult for the body to cope with all of the sugar. They can get a disease called diabetes.

Study the diagram. What might have caused the blockage in the artery?

What advice would you give a person with this kind of blockage about their diet?

■ For more activities, go to Workbook 4 page 76.

Obesity

Obesity means being very overweight.

Being obese makes it more likely that the person will suffer from one or more of the following diseases:

- type 2 diabetes
- heart disease
- breast and bowel cancer
- stroke (a blocked blood vessel in the brain).

Obesity is caused by eating too much food, especially sugary and fatty foods, and not taking enough exercise.

Interviewing a health professional

Your teacher will invite a doctor, nurse, dietician or nutritionist into school to talk to you about a healthy diet.

1. Work with your group to decide on three questions you want to ask the health professional.

> Discuss your questions with the class.
>
> From all the questions discussed, decide on the five most important questions to ask.

2. During the talk take careful notes. At the end of the talk some of you will ask the questions. Remember to thank your visitor.

3. Write a letter to the visitor. Thank them again and write down the main points you learned from their talk.

Stretch zone

Design a leaflet for a hospital waiting room. Explain why adults should exercise and eat healthily to avoid obesity. Draw pictures too. Think about all the things you have learned about exercise and healthy eating.

Science fact

The World Health Organisation has shown that in 2016 there were over 650 000 000 adults and 378 000 000 children that were obese. These figures are rising as more and more people eat sugary and fatty foods and take less exercise.

Key idea

Eating too much fatty and sugary food can be harmful to our health.

■ For more activities, go to Workbook 4 page 77.

Looking after teeth

In this lesson you will find out that some foods can be harmful to your teeth.

Key words

plaque
toothbrush
tooth decay

Think back

Which foods can be harmful and lead to obesity and type 2 diabetes if we eat too much of them?

A dentist looks after our teeth. A dentist usually tells us to not eat too many sweet foods and drinks because they are bad for our teeth.

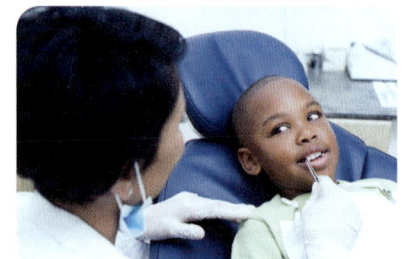

Do you go to the dentist?
Discuss with your partner what happens when you go to the dentist.

Do sweet drinks damage our teeth?

You are going to use small pieces of rock to model teeth. The rocks are made of a similar material to your teeth.

1 Place small amounts of marble or limestone in different drinks. Use water, apple juice, lemonade and cola. Label the containers with the names of the liquids you use.

2 Leave the rock pieces in the containers for about two weeks. After the two weeks, take out each piece, dry it and look at it carefully.

3 Record your observations. Draw a picture of each rock at the start of the investigation and after two weeks in the liquid.

Why did you use pieces of rock?

Which drinks caused the most damage to the rocks? What does this tell you about the effects of some drinks on your teeth?

Be a scientist

Scientists control their investigations. They need to find out what would happen if nothing changed in an investigation. That is why you added one piece of rock to water.

▶ page 8

When we drink sugary drinks, the sugars change to acids in our mouths. Acids are chemicals that attack and break down our teeth. Teeth can get a build up of a material called plaque. This can also damage teeth. When teeth are broken down, this is called tooth decay.

■ For more activities, go to Workbook 4 page 78.

Looking after your teeth

There are some very important things you can do to look after your teeth.

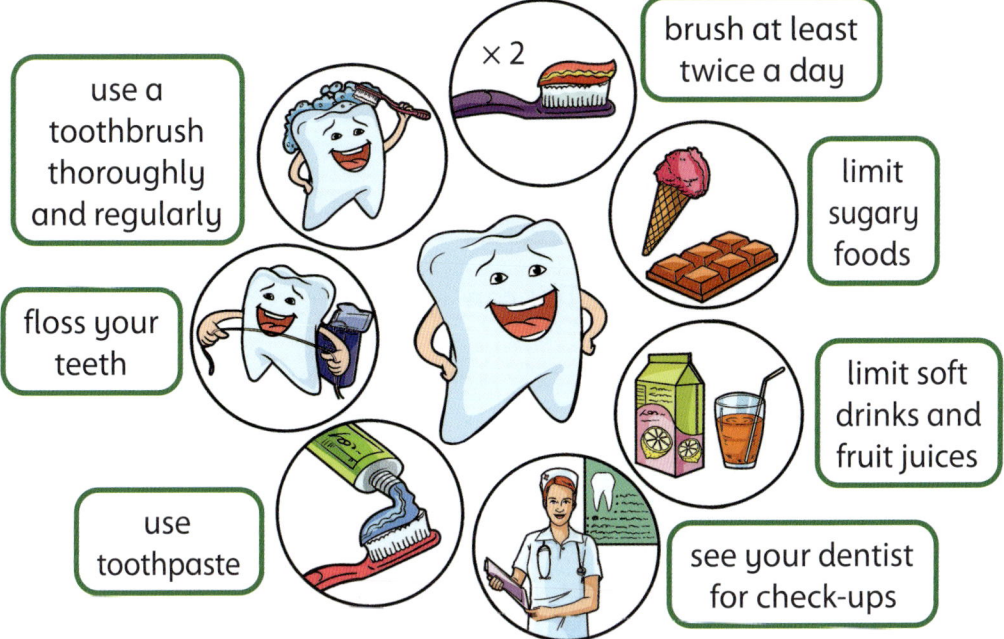

use a toothbrush thoroughly and regularly

brush at least twice a day

× 2

limit sugary foods

floss your teeth

limit soft drinks and fruit juices

use toothpaste

see your dentist for check-ups

Advising people how to look after their teeth

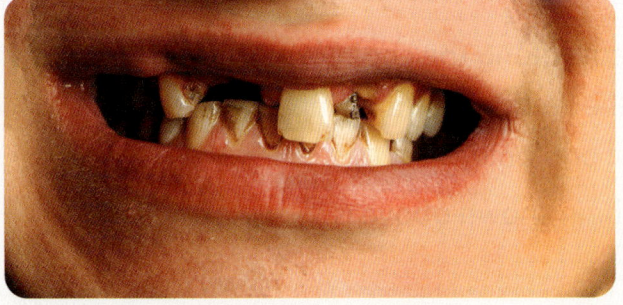

1   Look at the photograph of the teeth.
    How could the person have looked after their teeth better?
2   Write an e-mail to the person giving them advice about what to eat and what not to eat.

We need to look after our teeth because when we have our adult teeth, we do not grow any more teeth.

We use our teeth to chew our food so we can digest it more easily. Without teeth we would have to eat liquid food.

Key idea

We should look after our teeth. This means not eating too many sugary foods or drinking too many sugary or acidic drinks, and regular cleaning.

■ For more activities, go to Workbook 4 page 79.

Food chains

In this lesson you will find out how food chains are used to show feeding relationships.

Key words
energy
food chain
habitat

Think back

Why does this bird need to eat?

What does the caterpillar eat?

A feeding relationship shows us what each animal eats. This can be plants or other animals.

Animals eat plants and other animals and the way this happens is shown in a food chain.

What do food chains tell us?

Food chains tell us what each animal eats along the chain. We use arrows to give information about the feeding relationships in a habitat. A habitat is where an animal or plant lives.

The feeding relationship for the food chain shown above is:

- Plants provide food for insects:

    plant – – ➤ insect

- Insects provide food for lizards:

    insect – – ➤ lizard

- Lizards provide food for snakes:

    lizard – – ➤ snake

Joined together, these relationships form a food chain:

plants – – ➤ insects – – ➤ lizards – – ➤ snakes

The arrows in food chains show the direction that energy is passed along the chain.

Look at the picture of a food chain. What do you think it tells us?

What types of living things do all of the food chains start with?

Where do these living things get their energy from?

■ For more activities, go to Workbook 4 page 80.

Science fact

Not all of the energy can be passed along a food chain. Most is lost through the living things moving or materials not being digested.

Be a scientist

Scientists observe living things very carefully. They do not disturb them and they make notes about everything they see.

▶ page 9

Looking for food chains

Your teacher will take you to a local area to observe the animals and plants you can find there.

1   Use books or the internet to help you to identify the living things you find.

2   Make a note of what the living things are eating, if you can observe this.

3   Identify one food chain. It must start with a plant.

4   Draw your food chain as a large poster. Include drawings or downloaded pictures. Remember to draw the arrows showing the energy being passed along.

How many living things are in this photograph?

With a partner, draw a food chain to show the feeding relationships in this desert ecosystem.

Key idea

Food chains can be used to show feeding relationships. Arrows show the direction of energy through the chain.

Stretch zone

Draw a food chain that you are in. Use words, arrows and pictures. Think about what you eat. Where does this food come from?

■ For more activities, go to Workbook 4 page 81.

Making food webs

In this lesson you will find out that feeding relationships often form larger food webs.

Key words

ecosystem
food web
habitat

Look at the diagram of a food web. How is it different from a food chain?

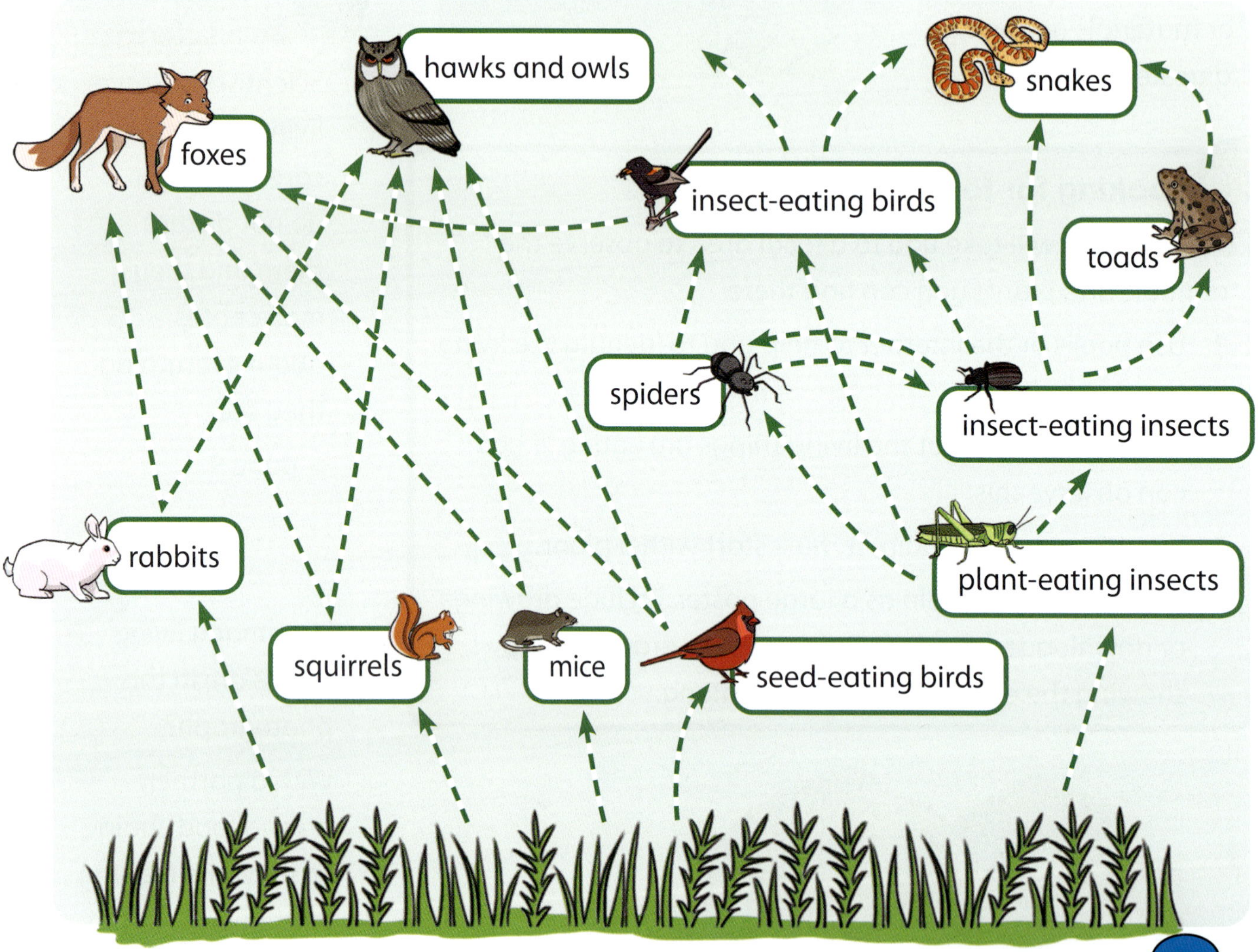

foxes

hawks and owls

snakes

insect-eating birds

toads

spiders

insect-eating insects

rabbits

plant-eating insects

squirrels

mice

seed-eating birds

Food webs give us more information. The feeding relationships are still shown by the arrows, but now there are more arrows.

A food web shows all the different things that animals eat in a habitat. For example, an owl does not only eat rabbits. It may eat a bird or a squirrel or a mouse sometimes. Food webs show all the feeding relationships in a habitat.

A habitat and all the living things in it, which interact in food webs, is called an ecosystem.

What types of living things are at the start of all of the food chains in the food web?

Why is there not an arrow pointing from the fox to the rabbit?

82

■ For more activities, go to Workbook 4 page 82.

Coral reef ecosystem

Rainforest ecosystem

Researching a food web

Your teacher will put you into different groups.

1. Use books, the internet or other sources to find out about a food web. This could be in a coral reef ecosystem, a rainforest ecosystem or a desert ecosystem (see page 81).

2. Split your group into three smaller expert groups. Each expert group then studies one of the ecosystems.

3. Meet back to share your information and ideas.

4. Work together to make an information leaflet to tell people about your food webs. Include drawings or downloaded pictures or photographs.

Be a scientist

Scientists use lots of different sources of information in their research. This allows them to think about different scientific evidence and views.

▶ page 8

Key idea

Food chains are often part of larger food webs in an ecosystem.

3 Digestion and Food Chains

83

■ For more activities, go to Workbook 4 page 83.

Green plants and sunlight

In this lesson you will learn that food chains begin with a plant (the producer), which uses energy from the Sun.

Key words

energy

producer

Sun

Think back

Plants can make their own food using energy from the Sun. Do you remember what else plants need to grow?

Look at the photographs of a healthy plant and an unhealthy plant.

Discuss which plant is healthy and which plant is unhealthy. What evidence did you see and use?

Why do plants need sunlight?

1 You will be given a plant. It has been in the dark for two days.

   Cover some of the leaves with silver foil. You can even cut shapes if you wish.

2 Leave the plant in the sunlight for a few hours.

3 Remove a leaf that has been covered and a leaf that has not been covered.

4 The leaves need to be added to very hot water. Blot the leaves dry with a paper towel.

5 Add two drops of iodine solution to each dried leaf.

6 Observe what happens. Record your findings.

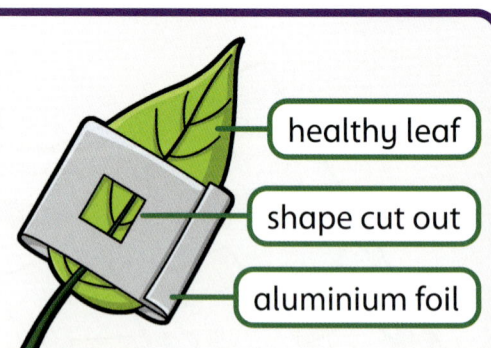

healthy leaf

shape cut out

aluminium foil

Warning! Be careful with hot water. Your teacher may add the leaves for you. Do not touch the iodine solution.

■ For more activities, go to Workbook 4 page 84.

When iodine is added to a material called starch it turns purple. Starch is how sugars are stored in leaves.

If you found starch in a leaf, it means the leaf has been able to make sugars.

The covered part of the leaf did not have any light energy reaching it and no starch was made.

This investigation shows that plants need sunlight to make sugars. Green plants can make their own food using the energy from sunlight.

 Stretch zone

Why was the plant left in the dark for a few days before the investigation?

Producers

When plants are healthy and can use energy from the Sun to make their own food, we call them producers. A producer can provide food for insects and animals.

Food chains always start with producers. Here are some examples.

Discuss why the leaf has a purple square shape on it.

How does this show why sunlight is important to green plants?

List the animals that eat plants. List the animals that eat other animals.

Discuss why the food chains start with a producer.

Key idea

The Sun provides energy for plants to make their own food. Plants are producers.

3 Digestion and Food Chains

85

■ For more activities, go to Workbook 4 page 85.

Passing energy along

In this lesson you will learn that energy is passed along food chains and webs and toxins can damage them.

Key words

energy
pyramid of numbers
toxins

Think back

Where do green plants get their energy from? What is the word used to describe green plants in food chains?

All living things need food because it provides the energy they need to live. We have looked at food chains and food webs. They all start with green plants called producers. Animals cannot make their own food. They have to eat something to get the energy they need. Animals are called consumers.

What happens to the energy?

Some of the energy is used by the animal. The rest of the energy is passed along the food chains and webs.

A food chain only shows one type of animal or plant at each level. Look at this example:

leaves - - ➤ giraffe - - ➤ lion

The giraffe needs lots of energy. It feeds on many trees and green plants. A lion will need to eat many giraffes and similar animals to stay alive.

We can get clues about how the energy is passed along food chains or webs. We show the living things as a pyramid or triangle.

Science fact

Each lion kills about 15 large animals each year. They also eat animals caught by other animals.

Look at the pyramid of numbers. Count the giraffes and lions. Discuss why the lion needs so many giraffes in the food chain.

Stretch zone

Find out what would happen if too many lions entered the area where the giraffes live.

■ For more activities, go to Workbook 4 page 86.

It is not only energy that is passed along a food chain or web. Nutrients in the plants and animals that are eaten are also passed on. If a poison, called a toxin, enters the food chain or web this can also be passed along.

Consumers further along the chain or web eat lots of organisms. If each of these organisms has some toxin, the consumers can end up taking in a large amount of toxin. This can kill them.

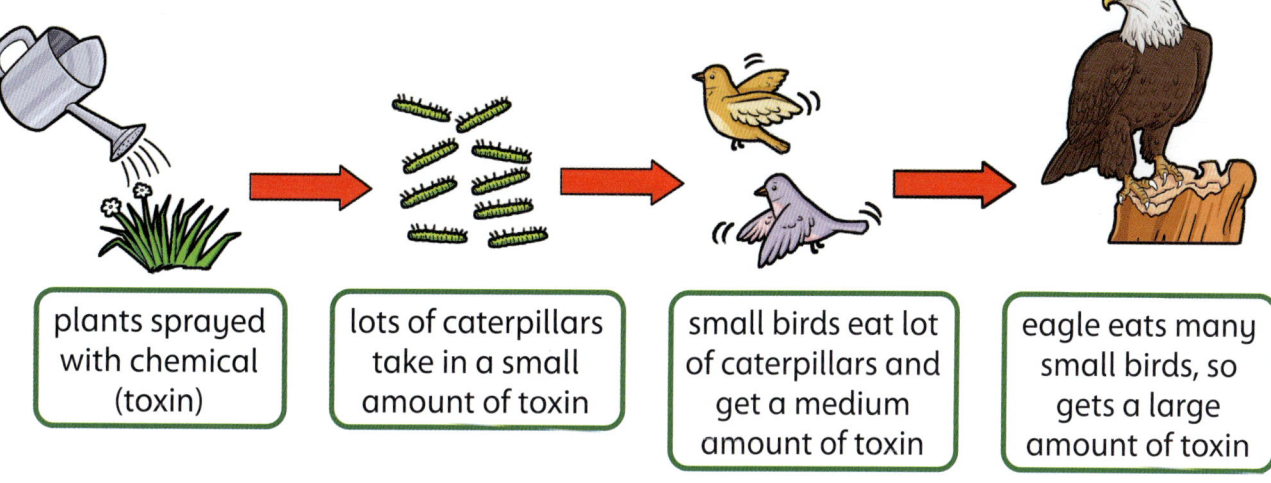

| plants sprayed with chemical (toxin) | lots of caterpillars take in a small amount of toxin | small birds eat lot of caterpillars and get a medium amount of toxin | eagle eats many small birds, so gets a large amount of toxin |

The amount of toxin can increase along the food chain

 Modelling a pyramid of numbers

You are going to make a pyramid model.

1 Count how many levels the pyramid has.

2 Decide how many living things you will put in each level of the pyramid.

3 Make a model pyramid. You can copy and use the outline shown. Cut out the shape and glue together.

4 Draw in your levels and the animals and plants found there. Make some information cards too. Display your model.

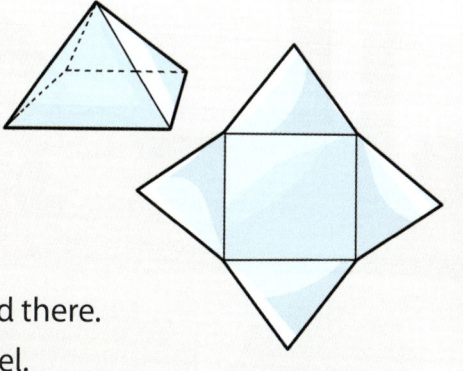

Key ideas

- We can use pyramids of numbers to model how energy flows through food chains and webs.
- Toxins can enter a food chain and damage living things.

■ For more activities, go to Workbook 4 page 87.

Producers and consumers

In this lesson you will learn about producers and consumers.

We know that plants use energy from the Sun to produce their own food. Now let's look more closely at the next stage in a food chain. Remember that animals cannot make their own food.

We call animals consumers because they eat plants or other animals.

What is the insect in the photograph doing? Is the insect a producer? Discuss your answer with a partner.

Look at the pictures of the plants and animals on this page. Identify which are producers and which are consumers. Make a table to record your ideas with your partner.

■ For more activities, go to Workbook 4 page 88.

Different types of consumer

In a food chain there may be different types of consumer. This depends upon how many plants and animals are in the chain.

Look at the food chain opposite.

We give special names to each consumer in this food chain:

1 Primary consumer – these animals eat plants. They are also known as herbivores. In this example it is the insect.

2 Secondary consumer – these animals eat the animals that eat plants. In this example it is the lizard.

3 Tertiary consumer – these animals eat the animals that have eaten herbivores. In this example it is the snake.

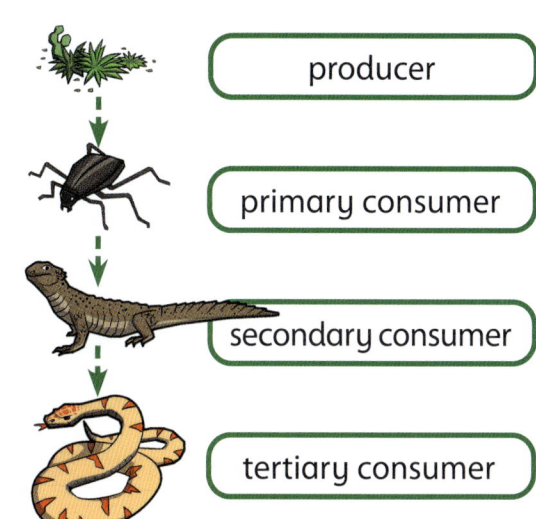

producer

primary consumer

secondary consumer

tertiary consumer

Identifying producers and consumers

You are going to make a model of the food chain using paper plates.

Look at the picture of the eagle on the opposite page. The eagle represents another level in the food chain – the quaternary consumer.

1 Use a different plate for each level of the food chain. Draw and name the living things.

2 On the back of the plate write if the living thing is a producer, primary consumer, secondary consumer, tertiary consumer or quaternary consumer.

3 Hang your plates from the ceiling of the classroom or a corridor. Make sure they are in the correct sequence. As the plates spin you will be able to see the living thing and to which level of the food chain it belongs.

Stretch zone

Research a food chain with five levels. Draw your food chain and label it clearly.

Key ideas

- Producers use energy from the Sun to provide food for consumers.
- There may be many levels of consumers.

3 Digestion and Food Chains

89

■ For more activities, go to Workbook 4 page 89.

Predators and prey

In this lesson you will learn about predators and prey.

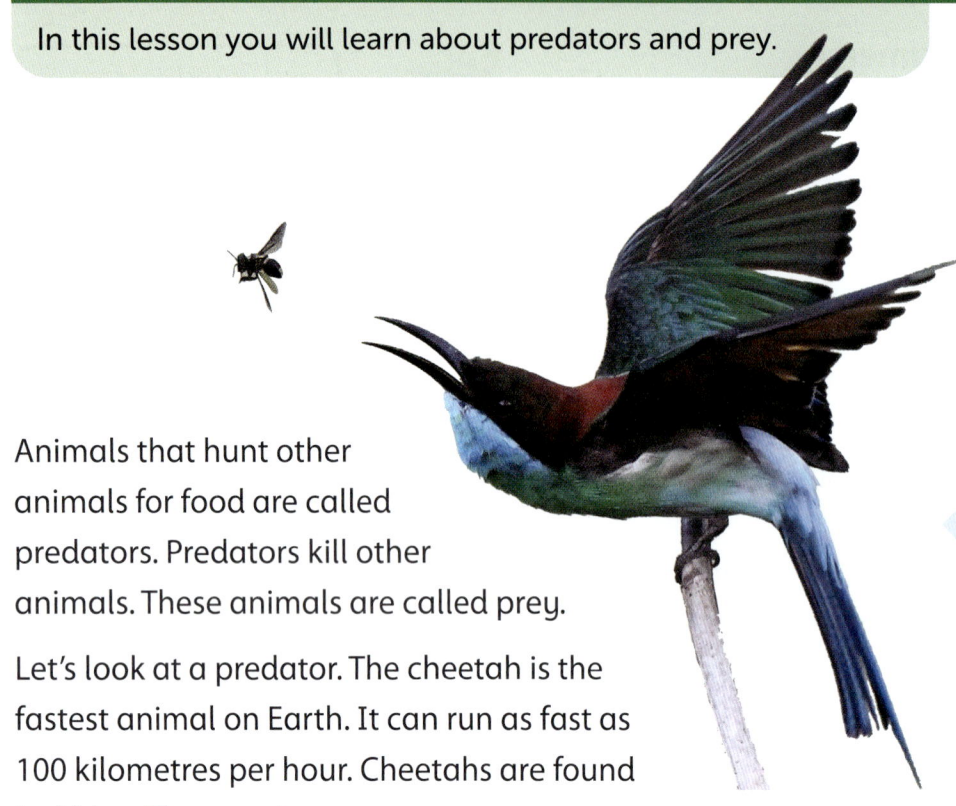

Key words

adaptation
predator
prey

Look at the photograph of the bird and insect. With a partner, discuss the names of three other animals that kill animals for food.

Animals that hunt other animals for food are called predators. Predators kill other animals. These animals are called prey.

Let's look at a predator. The cheetah is the fastest animal on Earth. It can run as fast as 100 kilometres per hour. Cheetahs are found in Africa. They are hunters.

Remember that adaptation is when an animal is suited to its habitat. Talk with a partner about how cheetahs are adapted to catch and eat gazelles, and how gazelles are adapted to escape.

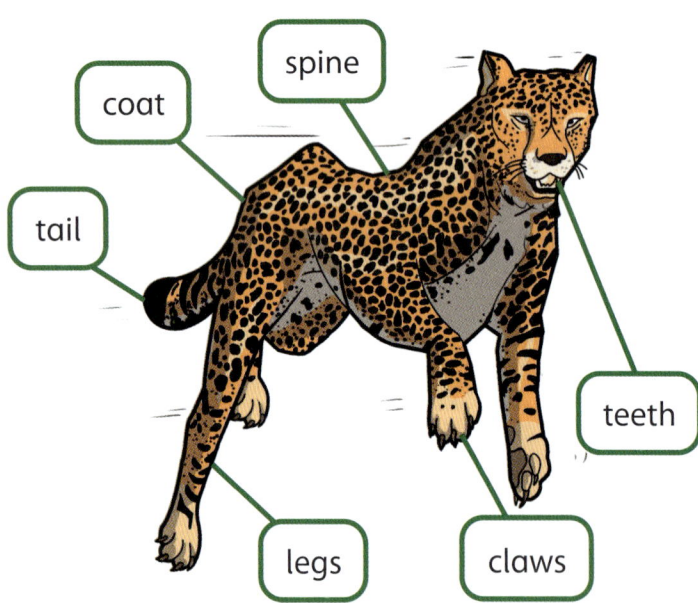

spine

coat

tail

teeth

legs

claws

horns

legs

eyes

Here is an example of prey. The gazelle can be found in Africa and Asia. It can run fast. Gazelles mainly eat green plants. They are hunted by lions, leopards, cheetahs and hyenas.

■ For more activities, go to Workbook 4 page 90.

Some animals blend into the background. They may look like leaves or tree bark. Their markings can make them hard to see. This is called camouflage. This is one example of an animal adaptation.

Can you find the animal hidden in the photograph?

Hiding from predators

You are going to make a model of a camouflaged animal.

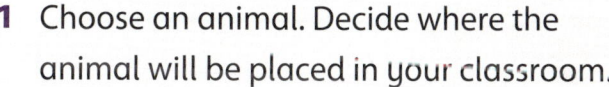

1 Choose an animal. Decide where the animal will be placed in your classroom.

2 Draw your animal onto card or paper. Colour in your animal to match the background so that it is camouflaged.

3 Place your animal drawing in the room. Ask others in your class to find your animal. How well camouflaged was it?

4 Work with the people in your class to make a wall display about how animals can hide from predators.

Stretch zone

Research how spines, horns, hard shells, large size and speed can help prey to escape predators. For each one of these features, write down an animal that uses this method.

Check how much you know.
Try the questions on pages 92–93.

Key ideas

- Some animals are predators. They hunt other animals, which are called prey.
- Camouflage is the way animals blend into their backgrounds.

■ For more activities, go to Workbook 4 page 91.

1 Arrange the food chain below into the correct order by drawing a line from the living thing to its box.

2 Label the diagram of the digestive system. Use the words in the word box.

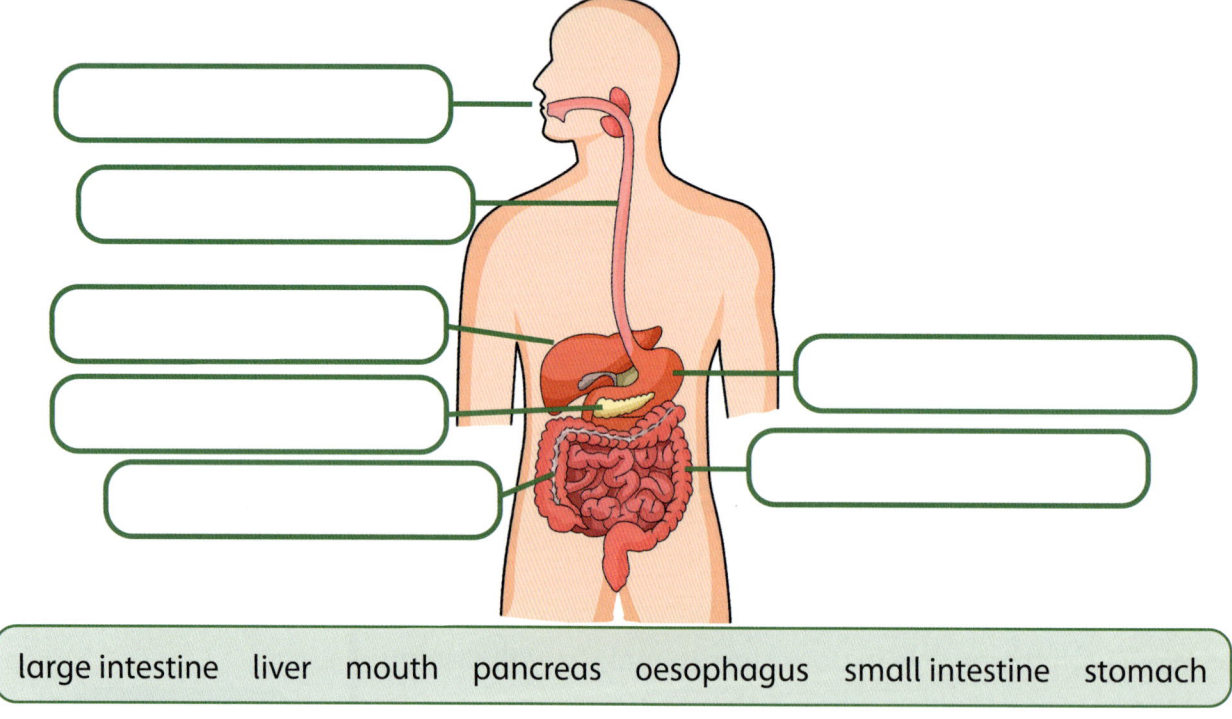

large intestine   liver   mouth   pancreas   oesophagus   small intestine   stomach

3 Identify the types and function of teeth. Draw a line from the function to the correct tooth name. Then draw a line from the name of the tooth to the correct picture.

cut food   tear food   crush food   grind food

molar   canine   incisor   pre-molar

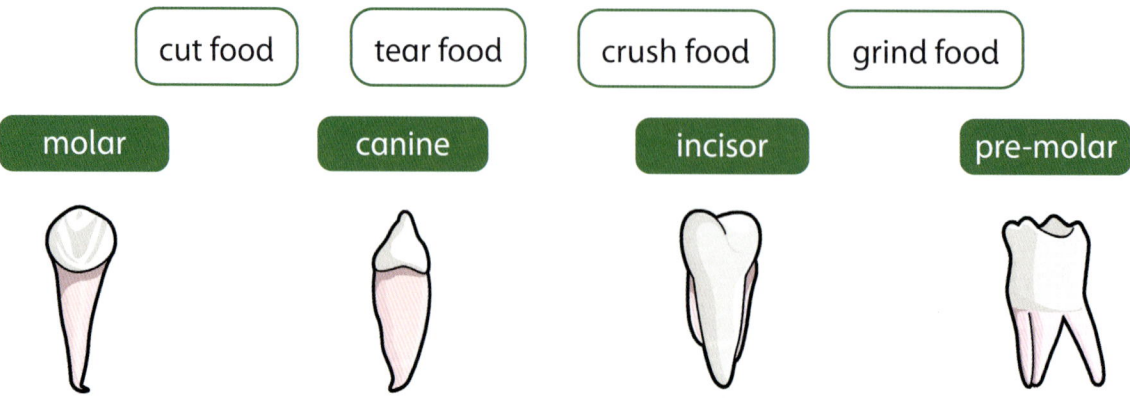

■ For more activities, go to Workbook 4 page 92.

4 Explain why plants are called producers.

_____

_____

5 Dieticians put foods into groups.

a Name three foods that are proteins.

_____   _____   _____

b Name three foods that are carbohydrates.

_____   _____   _____

6 Study the food web below.

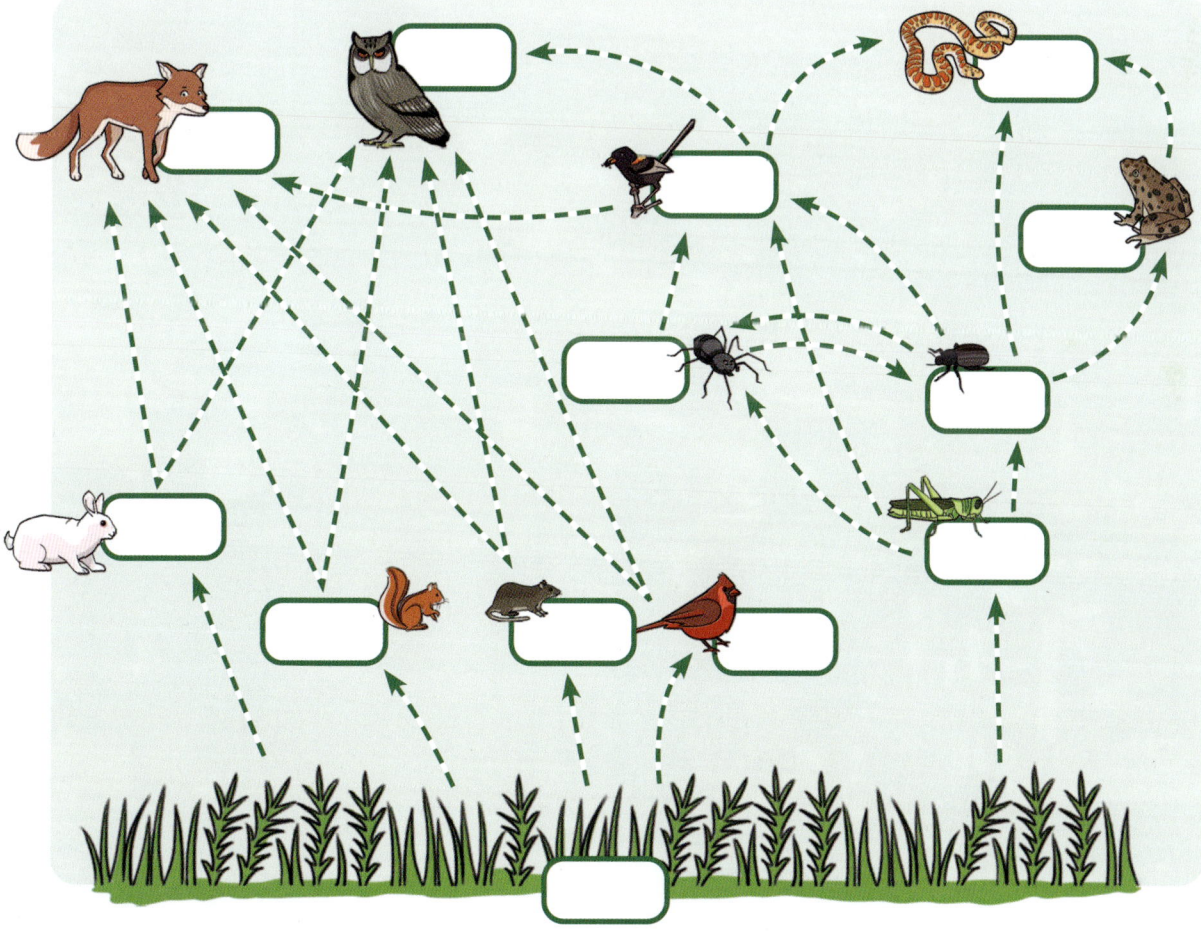

Colour the box of any producers in green.
Colour the box of any primary consumers in brown.
Colour the box of any secondary consumers in red.
Colour the box of any tertiary consumers in blue.

■ For more activities, go to Workbook 4 page 93.

4 Electricity

In this unit you will:

- explore appliances that run on electricity
- find out what parts make simple electric circuits work
- construct electric circuits
- explore how to use a switch to break a circuit
- discover some common conductors and insulators
- understand how to be safe with electricity.

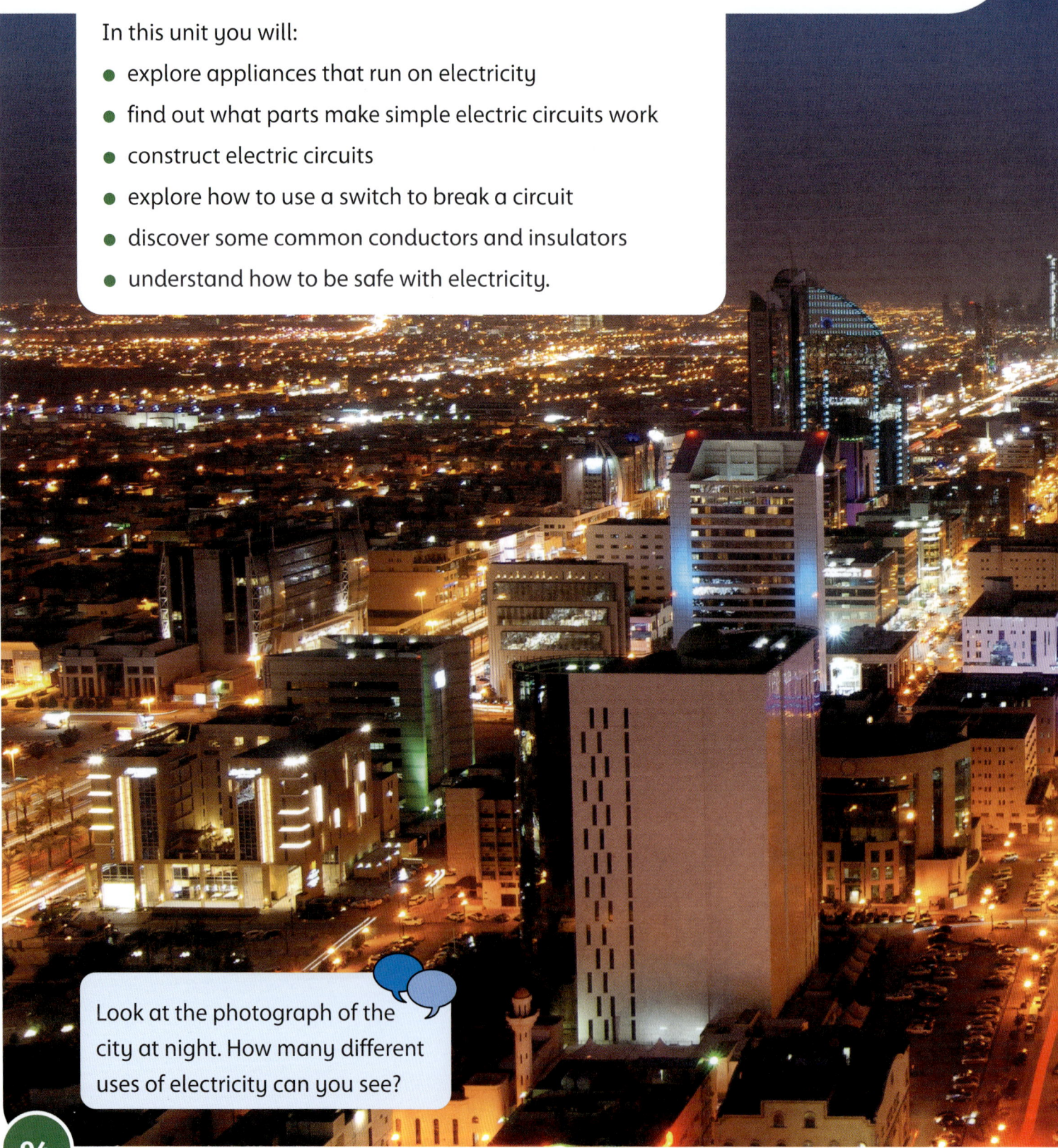

Look at the photograph of the city at night. How many different uses of electricity can you see?

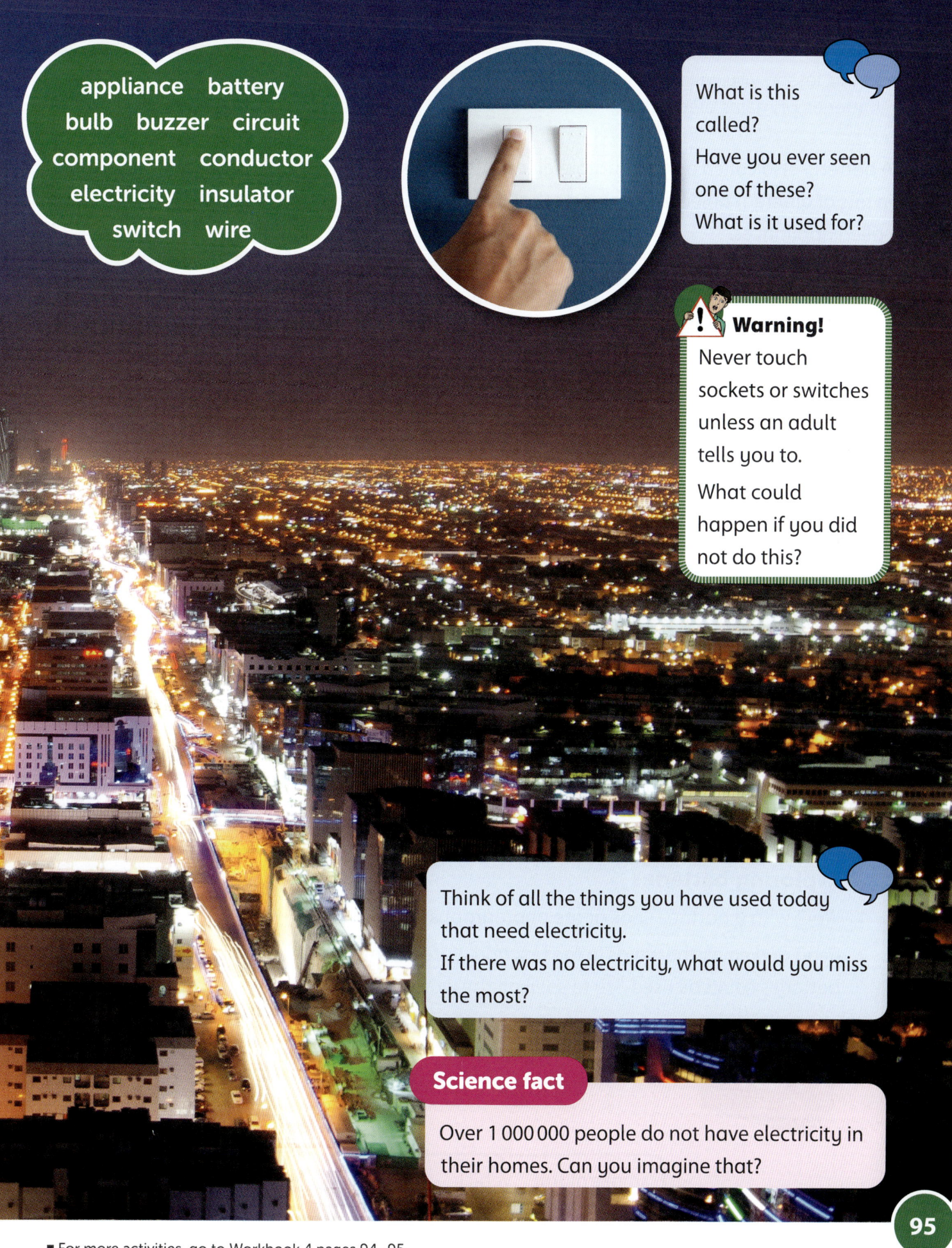

appliance   battery
bulb   buzzer   circuit
component   conductor
electricity   insulator
switch   wire

What is this called?
Have you ever seen one of these?
What is it used for?

Warning!

Never touch sockets or switches unless an adult tells you to.

What could happen if you did not do this?

Think of all the things you have used today that need electricity.
If there was no electricity, what would you miss the most?

Science fact

Over 1 000 000 people do not have electricity in their homes. Can you imagine that?

■ For more activities, go to Workbook 4 pages 94–95.

Electricity supply

In this lesson you will find out that appliances can be run by batteries or mains electricity.

Key words
appliance
battery
electricity
plug
wire

A battery, also called a cell, can store electricity. We use batteries in lots of different objects. The objects that use electricity are called appliances.

Look around the room. Can you see any appliances that might be using batteries?

You might have thought about a torch or a battery-operated toy.

Did you know that bigger appliances use batteries? The vehicles in the photograph use batteries.

There are many different shapes and sizes of battery. Watches and hearing aids use really tiny batteries. Vehicles have much bigger batteries.

Are vehicles appliances? Discuss your thoughts with a partner.

Exploring batteries

1 Work with a partner. Look at the photographs below.

2 Read and cover the words in the box and write a sentence about where each of the batteries could be used. Try to spell all the words in the sentence correctly.

smoke alarm   vehicle   watch

■ For more activities, go to Workbook 4 page 96.

The biggest batteries in the world are bigger than a football pitch. They make enough electricity for 12 000 homes for one hour. That's a lot of electricity!

When you put a plug into a socket the electricity is provided by the mains.

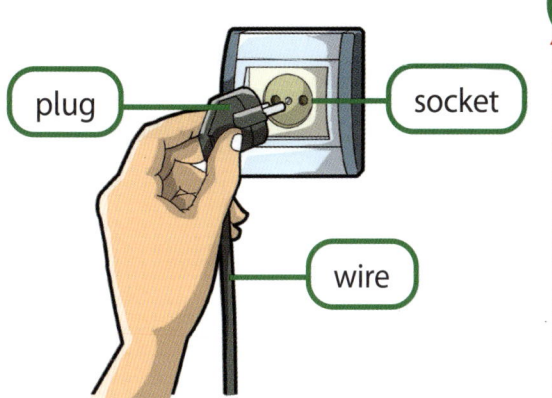

plug

socket

wire

Warning!

Mains electricity is dangerous. Do not put anything into an electrical socket, even if you think it is switched off. Discuss why this is important.

Is there mains electricity in your classroom?

Do you know other places where there is mains electricity?

Appliance survey

You are going to survey the appliances in your school to identify if they are run by battery or mains electricity.

1 Look around the school to identify appliances that need electricity to work. Make a list.

2 Design a table to identify which appliances run on batteries and which need mains electricity.

3 Make a poster to present your results. Include drawings or photographs of some of the appliances.

4 Which appliance would you miss the most if electricity did not exist?

Key ideas

- Batteries and mains can give us electricity.
- Mains electricity can be dangerous so you need to be careful when using it.

Stretch zone

Why would we sometimes choose to use batteries instead of mains for electricity? Discuss with your partner.

4 Electricity

97

■ For more activities, go to Workbook 4 page 97.

Making circuits

In this lesson you will build a simple series circuit.

Think back

Remember: things that use electricity are called appliances.

Key words
battery
bulb
circuit
component
connector
wire

Electricity has to flow in a complete pathway. Everything has to be joined together in a circle for the parts to work. This is called a circuit.

Look at page 97. What is connected to a plug?

What does this do in a circuit?

battery

wires

bulb

Wires carry the electricity from a battery, or the mains, to all the different parts of a circuit. The parts of a circuit are called components.

In a wire, the electricity moves along the material at the centre. The outer covering stops the electricity from moving into you.

Looking at wires

Your teacher will give you and your partner a wire to look at.

1 What is the material around the wire?

2 What is the material inside this?

3 What do you think would happen if you bent or twisted the wire too much?

If a wire breaks, the electricity cannot flow to the components.

■ For more activities, go to Workbook 4 page 98.

Building a circuit

Work with a partner. Your teacher will give you a bulb, a battery, connectors and wires. These are the components of your circuit.

1 Connect the bulb, wires and battery together using connectors to make a circuit.
2 Make sure everything is properly connected.
3 What happens to the bulb?

 Warning!

Be careful when you use connectors. They can sometimes be very sharp and nip your skin.

If the bulb lights up, all the parts of the circuit are working and you have done everything correctly. This kind of circuit is known as a simple series circuit.

Some materials do not allow electricity to flow through them but others do. Wires are made from materials that let electricity pass through them easily. They are called conductors.

Investigating different materials

You will investigate which materials let electricity run through them. Work with a partner. Your teacher will give you some objects to test.

1 Predict which materials will conduct electricity.
2 Make a circuit like the one in the diagram. Use a different kind of material each time, in place of the spoon.
3 Write down the materials that lit the bulb.

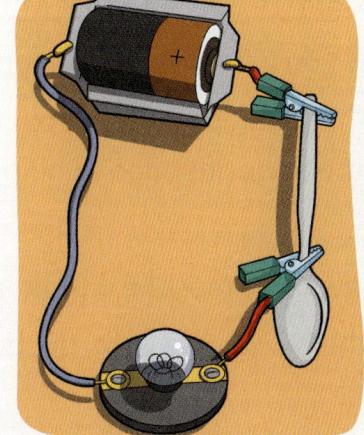

 Be a scientist

Scientists make predictions based on what they already know.

▶ page 7

Key ideas

- Wires carry electricity around a circuit.
- Not all materials allow electricity to pass through.

If the bulb lights up, this means the material is letting electricity flow through it to complete the circuit.

If the bulb does not light up, then the material is not letting electricity flow through it.

■ For more activities, go to Workbook 4 page 99.

Parts of a simple series circuit

In this lesson you will understand how to use different components in a simple series circuit.

Key words
battery
bulb
buzzer
wire

Think back

What do we call the parts of a circuit?

List as many of these as you can, that you have used so far to build circuits.

Electricity is not just used to give us light. There are other uses too. So sometimes you need other components in a circuit.

A buzzer can be one of them.

Making a buzzer work

You are going to build a simple circuit with these components.

   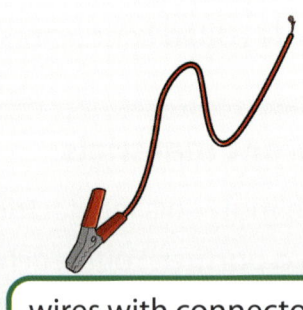 

| battery | bulb | wires with connectors | buzzer |

1 Agree with a partner how you will connect the components to make a simple circuit.

2 Connect all the parts of the circuit together. Draw the circuit in your notebook. You can use the diagram on the opposite page to help you.

3 Does the buzzer buzz?

4 If the buzzer does not buzz, there must be a fault in the circuit.

   To find out if the fault is the buzzer, the bulb, the battery or the connections, you need to set up a test circuit.

   The diagram opposite shows how to set up a test circuit. Use the diagram to make your own test circuit.

5 Test the components and wires from your buzzer circuit by placing one at a time in your test circuit.

6 Where was the fault?

■ For more activities, go to Workbook 4 page 100.

This simple test series circuit contains a bulb, a battery, connecting wires and connectors to test components.

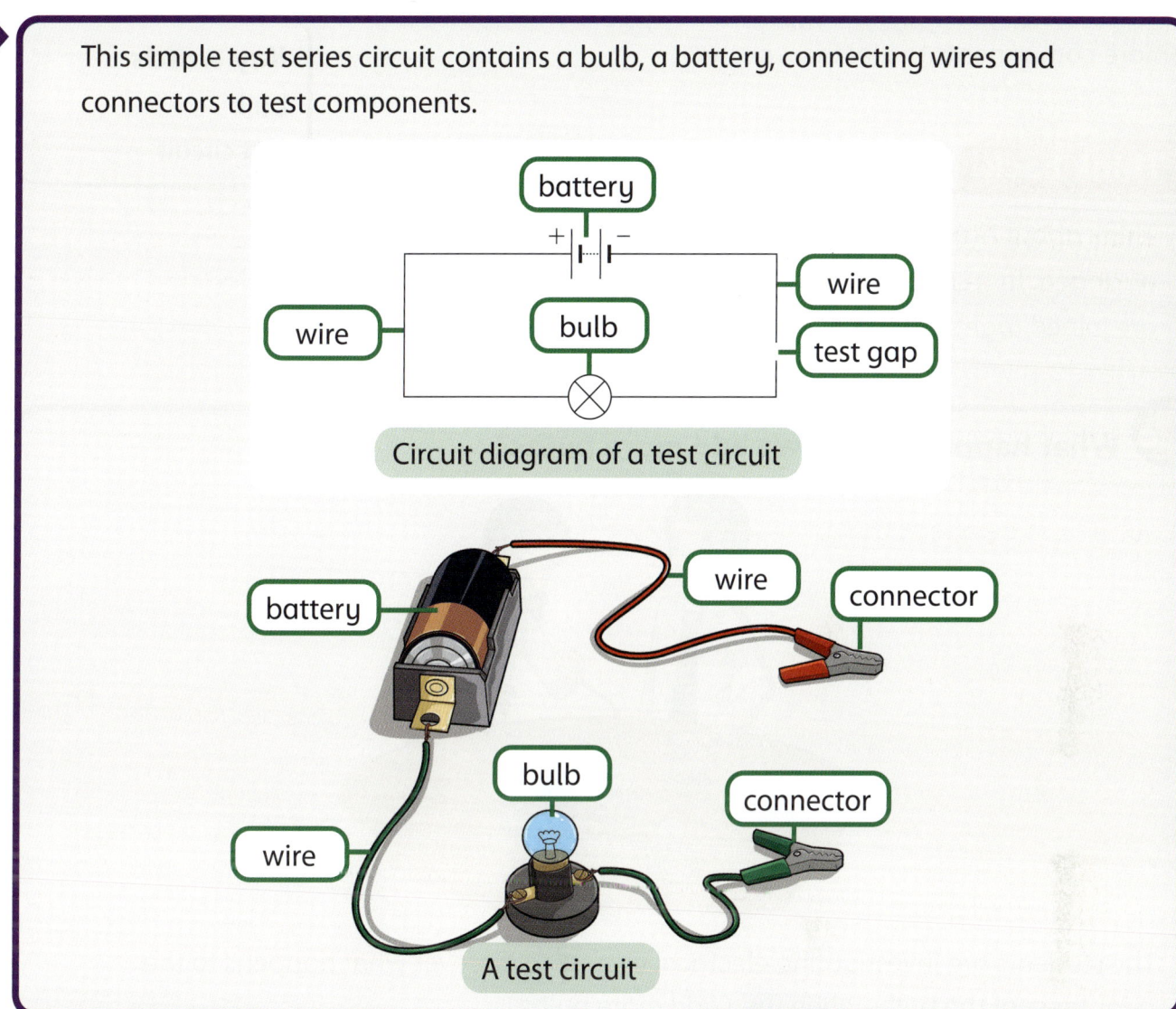

Circuit diagram of a test circuit

A test circuit

Can you think of any circuits which have buzzers?
Why do they?

When a buzzer is added to a circuit it makes a noise. This can attract our attention.

Doorbells, car horns and sirens are examples of this.

Stretch zone

Why do you think modern smoke alarms are connected to the mains but also have a battery? Explain your thinking to your partner.

Key idea

Wires, batteries, bulbs and buzzers can be components of a circuit.

■ For more activities, go to Workbook 4 page 101.

4 Electricity

More electrical components

In this lesson you will investigate what happens when you add more components to electrical circuits.

Key words
bulb
test circuit

Think back

Think about how the components in a circuit can be arranged. In a simple series circuit all of the components are joined together, one after the other.

What happens when we add more bulbs?

The students are investigating electrical circuits to discover what happens to the brightness of the bulbs when they add more bulbs.

1 With a partner, predict what will happen to the brightness of the bulbs as the students add more bulbs to the circuit.

2 Write down your prediction, with reasons.

3 Plan and carry out an investigation to find out.

4 Record your findings in a table like the one below.

Number of bulbs in circuit	Observation
I	the bulb is very bright

What could you change in the circuit to make the bulbs brighter?

5 Discuss with your partner what happened when you added more bulbs to the circuit. Write a conclusion for your investigation.

■ For more activities, go to Workbook 4 page 102.

What happens when we add more batteries?

1. Predict what happens when you add more batteries to this circuit.

2. Plan and carry out an investigation to test your prediction. Use three bulbs in your test circuit to make it a fair test.

3. Predict what would happen if you carried on increasing the number of batteries in the circuit.

4. Write a conclusion for this investigation.

What happens when we change the positions of the components?

1. Predict if circuit 1 or circuit 2 will have brighter bulbs.

circuit 1

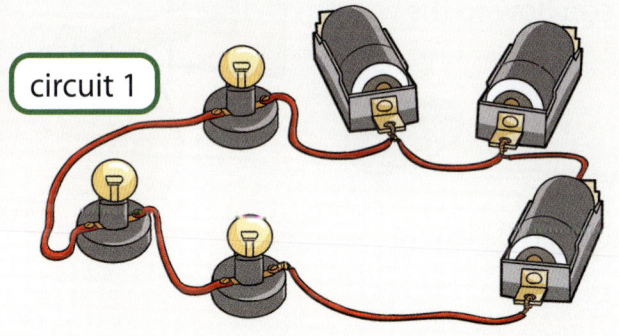

circuit 2

2. Construct the circuits to test your prediction.

3. Record your findings in a suitable table.

4. Study the table of results and write a conclusion about your investigation.

When the components were moved around the circuit, did the brightness of the bulbs change?

Stretch zone

Fairy lights are joined in a very long circuit. If one bulb stops working none of them will work.

Explain why this happens.

Key ideas

- We can add more components to a circuit.
- When we add more bulbs, the bulbs get less bright.

■ For more activities, go to Workbook 4 page 103.

4 Electricity

Using switches

In this lesson you will explore how a switch can be used to break a circuit.

Key words

circuit

switch

Sometimes it is useful to be able to switch some components off and on when you want to.

What happens to a circuit when there is a break in it?

Look at picture 1. Can you see that the switch is being turned off?

This makes a break in the circuit.

This means that electricity cannot flow over the gap to the device, so the device does not work.

Look at picture 2. Now the switch has been turned on.

This means that the break is closed. Electricity can flow to the device and it works.

Look at the picture below of a circuit with a switch.

There is a gap between the two pieces of metal in the switch.

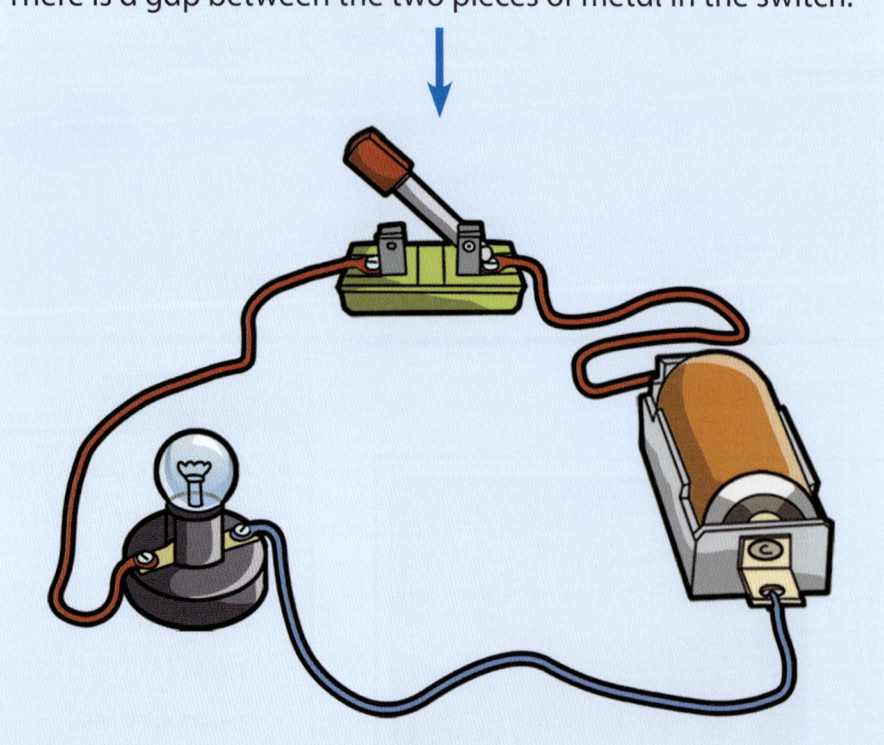

Is the switch in the picture on or off?

■ For more activities, go to Workbook 4 page 104.

Co...

Look c...

1 Pre...

2 Co...

A

Look carefully at this picture of a closed switch.

Is there a gap between the two pieces of metal?

Will the electricity flow through this switch if it is joined in a circuit?

Exploring how a switch works

You are going to explore how a switch works.

1 Make a simple circuit using the components you are given.

2 Add a switch to the circuit.

3 Predict what will happen when you press the switch on and then off.

4 Write down your predictions.

The materials used in a switch must allow electricity to flow through it.

Be a scientist

Scientists record their predictions and results in tables.

▶ page 11

Making a switch

1 Take the switch out of your circuit.

2 Put a paperclip in its place.

3 Slide the paperclip over to the loose crocodile clip.

4 What happens?

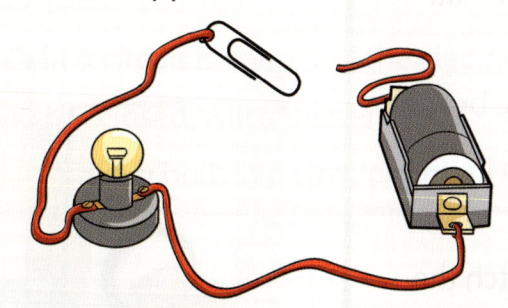

Does the paperclip work like a switch?

Does the bulb light in the same way as before?

Key idea

Switches can close or break a circuit. They are used to turn electrical appliances on and off.

Re...

Work ...

Const...

1 Wh...
wo...

2 Wh...

3 Wh...

4 Ho...

St...

There...

dimm...

findin...

Stretch zone

Why does the paperclip still light the bulb?

4 Electricity

105

1 **(a)** Label the components in this circuit.

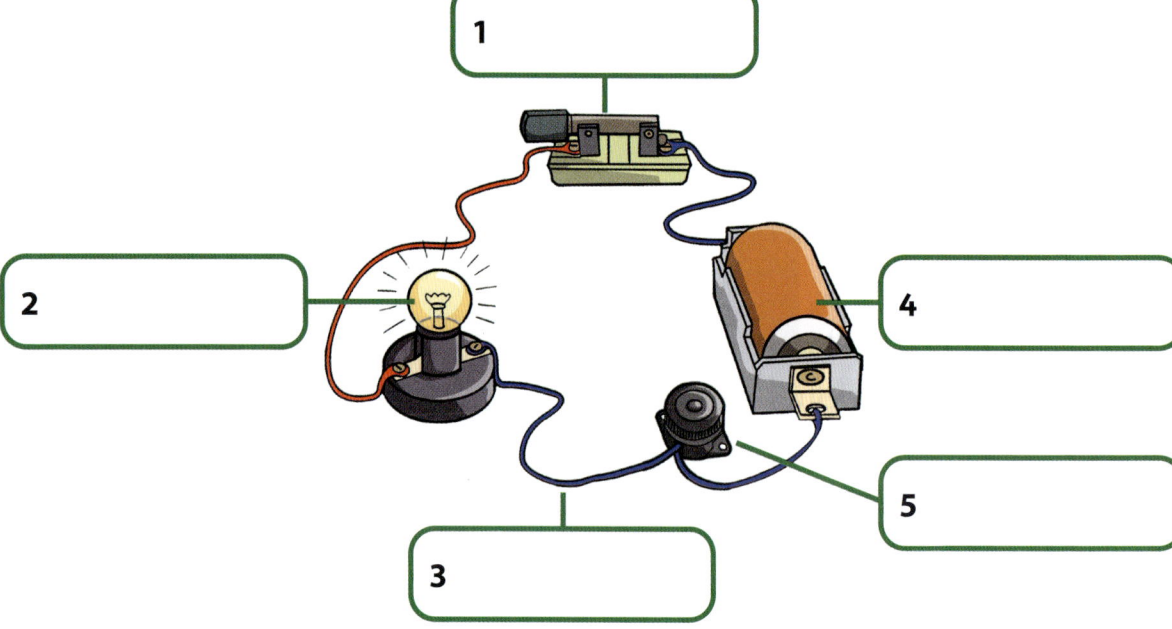

(b) Which component creates the electricity in the circuit? Tick this component.

(c) Cross out the word that is not a component of a circuit.

battery   bulb   toy   wire

2 Look back at the circuit diagram in question 1. What would happen to the bulb if another battery was added to the circuit? Circle the correct answer.

It would stay the same.   It would get brighter.   It would get dimmer.

3 **(a)** Which spoon will make the bulb light up in the test circuit? _____.

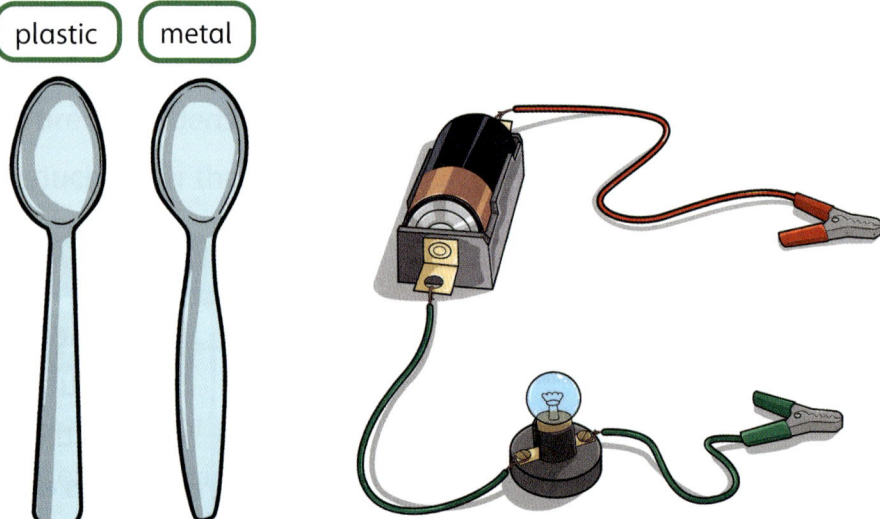

plastic   metal

■ For more activities, go to Workbook 4 page 114.

b Choose the correct word to complete the sentence:

conductor   insulator

The plastic spoon is a good _____.

The metal spoon is a good _____.

4 How can you find a fault in a series circuit?

_____

_____

5 Why is mains electricity much more dangerous than electricity from a battery?

_____

_____

_____

6 **a** Explain what happens when a circuit is broken.

_____

_____

b Which component do we use to break a circuit? _____

7 Why doesn't the buzzer buzz in this circuit?

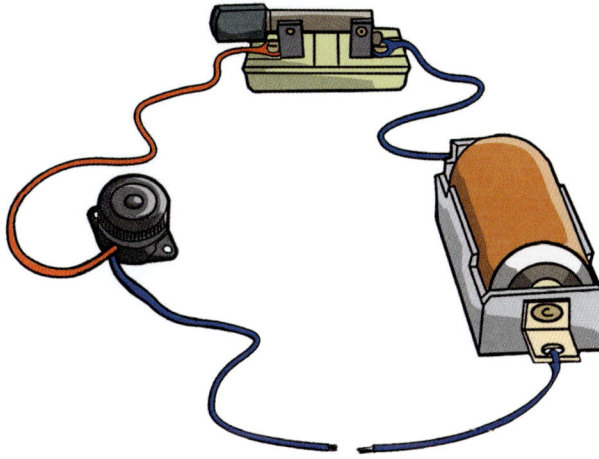

_____

_____

■ For more activities, go to Workbook 4 page 115.

5 Sounds

In this unit you will:

- explore how sounds are made and learn how to measure sound
- investigate how sound travels through different materials to the ear
- recognise that sounds get fainter as the distance from the sound source increases
- investigate patterns between high and low or loud and quiet sounds
- explore patterns in pitch of sounds and how we can change pitch.

Science fact

The African cicada is the loudest insect in the world. Scientists have measured the sound as 107 decibels.

A pneumatic drill makes about the same amount of sound!

What are the people wearing over their ears? Why?

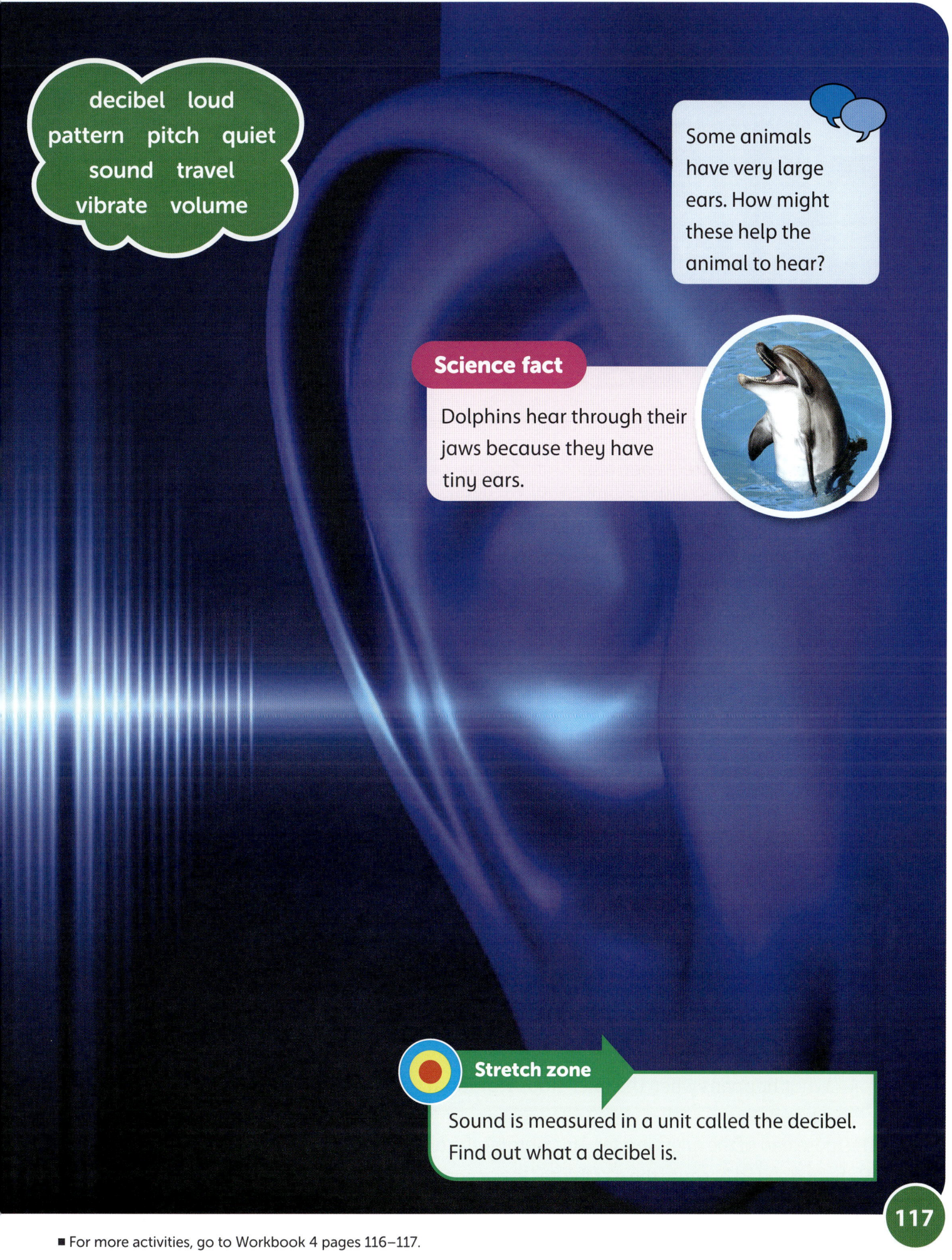

decibel loud
pattern pitch quiet
sound travel
vibrate volume

Some animals have very large ears. How might these help the animal to hear?

Science fact

Dolphins hear through their jaws because they have tiny ears.

Stretch zone

Sound is measured in a unit called the decibel. Find out what a decibel is.

■ For more activities, go to Workbook 4 pages 116–117.

How sounds are made

In this lesson you will explore how sounds are made.

Key words

sound

vibrate

What is sound?

There are lots of sounds around us. We can make sounds by talking, clapping our hands and whistling.

Cars, phones and TVs make sounds that we hear.

Sound can only happen if something moves backwards and forwards. We say it vibrates. When something vibrates, it makes the air or surrounding materials vibrate too.

The vibrations move across the air or material and reach the ear.

What can you hear?

1 Sit quietly. Listen to the sounds around you.

2 Describe the sounds you can hear.

3 What is making each sound?

Stretch zone

Choose one of the sounds. What is vibrating to make the sound?

We need vibrations to hear sounds

You will demonstrate that we need vibrations to hear sounds.

1 Hold a ruler on the edge of your desk with one hand.

2 With your other hand, pull the end of the ruler down and let it go.

3 What happens to the end of the ruler?

4 What happens when the ruler stops vibrating?

The loose end of the ruler vibrates. This vibrates the air around it. We hear a sound because the air vibrates in our ears. We can see the ruler vibrating up and down but we cannot see the air vibrating.

■ For more activities, go to Workbook 4 page 118.

How can we investigate the vibrations that cause sound?

1 Hit a drum with a stick or your hand.

2 Put rice on to the drum and then hit it.

3 What happens to the rice?

What causes this?

Musicians and singers use tuning forks. If you tap the end of the tuning fork it starts to vibrate.

How can we hear a sound from the tuning fork? How does the sound reach our ears?

Exploring tuning forks

1 Tap a tuning fork and put it on the rim of a container of water.

2 What can you see on the surface of the water?

This is the sound vibration moving through the water.

We hear a guitar because the string vibrates. The string vibrates the air as it moves to our ears.

How can we investigate this?

Make a guitar

Make a guitar like the one in the picture.

1 What happens when you pluck the string?

2 What does the vibrating string do to the air?

3 How does this make us hear the sound?

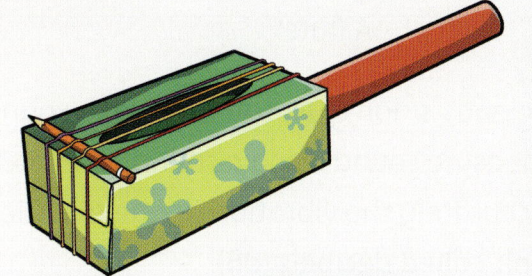

Stretch zone

How can you make your guitar sound louder or quieter?

Key idea

We hear sound when something vibrates.

■ For more activities, go to Workbook 4 page 119.

Observing and measuring sound

In this lesson you will learn how to describe and measure sound.

Key words
decibel
loud/quiet
volume

The volume of a sound is how loud or quiet it is. Some people say a sound gets fainter and others say it gets quieter. These are the same thing.

The more energy put into the vibration, the louder the sound will be.

Volume

1 Gently hit or pluck a musical instrument. Is the sound loud or quiet?

2 Now hit or pluck the instrument as hard as you can. What is the difference in sound?

Work with a partner and look at the photographs below.

Discuss which instrument could make the loudest sound. What other differences in sound might you notice? Write down any science ideas you used to help you decide your answers.

A flute

A tuba

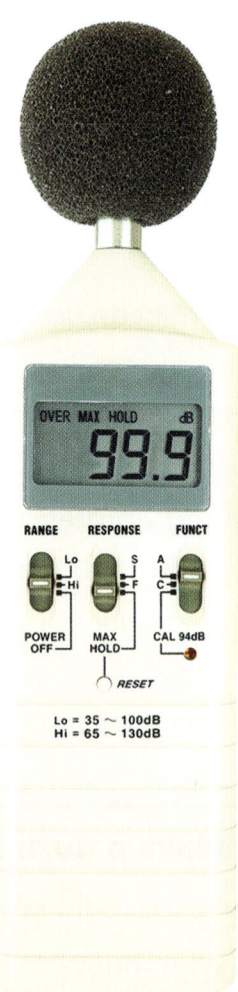

Scientists don't just say whether a sound is loud or quiet. They measure sound using a sound-level meter. It measures accurately the vibrations in the air. Scientists measure sound in a unit called decibels (dB).

Think back

Remember the other units of measurement that you have used. Kilometres is the unit for distance and Celsius is the unit for temperature.

Discuss the reading on this sound-level meter. Find out if this sound is loud or quiet.

120

■ For more activities, go to Workbook 4 page 120.

Sound levels in the school

1 Use a sound-level meter to measure the sound levels in your school.

2 Design a table like this to record your results.

Place	Sound level (dB)
canteen	65 dB

Discuss with your group why it is important to draw a table of results.

3 Which place do you predict will be the loudest? And the quietest?

4 What was the highest reading you took?

5 Why was this place so loud?

6 List three places that had a reading below 60 decibels (dB).

Humans cannot hear sounds that are below 0 dB.

If a sound is too loud it can be very painful. Sounds above 160 dB permanently damage our ears.

Scientists have made a list of different sound levels. This list helps us keep our hearing safe.

Warning!
Never listen to very loud sounds. What could happen if you did?

Type of sound	Sound level (dB)
rustling leaves	10
whisper	20
conversation	60
busy traffic	70
vacuum cleaner	80
music through headphones	100
a child screaming	110
causes humans pain	130
jet taking off	140
permanent damage to the ear	160

With a partner, predict the sound level in decibels of:

● a person shouting

● a feather falling.

Use secondary sources to find out if your predictions are correct.

Key idea

We measure the volume of sound in decibels (dB).

■ For more activities, go to Workbook 4 page 121.

How does sound travel to our ears?

In this lesson you will learn that sound needs a material to travel through to enter the ear.

Key words

material

travel

vacuum

Think back

How does sound travel to our ears?

Sound can travel through materials and air. When an object vibrates it makes the air or any material next to it vibrate also.

It is like playing skittles. When we hit one skittle with a ball, it knocks into the next skittle and that one knocks into the next skittle. Sound vibrations travel through materials and air in a similar way.

Sound can travel through lots of different materials.

Does sound travel well through all materials?

1 Draw a table of results like the one below.

2 Include all the objects you will test and the materials they are made of.

3 Write down what you hear. For example, stand with your ear against a wall. If you listen carefully you can hear sounds. This means that the vibrations are travelling through the wall and vibrating in your ear. The wall is probably made out of brick or stone. This means sound can travel through the brick and stone.

Object	Material	Sounds I heard
wall	bricks	talking, voices, children playing
window	glass	
door	wood	
curtain	cotton	

4 Test all the objects in your list. Record your results in your table.

Have you ever heard sounds from the room next door? What can you conclude about whether sound can travel through a wall?

■ For more activities, go to Workbook 4 page 122.

What happens to sound in a vacuum?

You have learned that sound needs a material to travel through. What happens to sound if there is no material to travel through?

bell jar

phone

vacuum pump

In a vacuum there is no material or air for vibrations to travel through. The photograph shows a bell jar. A vacuum pump sucks all the air out of the jar. The phone is ringing but we cannot hear it. This is because there is nothing to transmit the vibrations from the phone to our ears.

 Stretch zone

Where do the vibrations go?

Space is a vacuum, just like inside the bell jar.

The astronaut in the photograph Is working on a space ship.

Can he hear the sound he makes as he repairs the space ship?

Will the people inside the space ship hear the sound?

Key idea

Sounds need a material to travel through for us to hear them.

■ For more activities, go to Workbook 4 page 123.

5 Sounds

Investigating how sound travels

In this lesson you will investigate how sound travels through different materials to the ear.

Key words

material
pattern
transmit

Not all materials transmit sound in the same way. This is because sound vibrations move differently through different materials.

Which materials transmit sound the best?

Draw a table to help you record your observations from this investigation.

1 Work with a partner. Look around the room. Choose six materials to test.

2 Predict which material you think will transmit sound the best.

3 One person puts their ear against an object and the other whispers a word against the object.

  If you hear the correct word clearly, the material has transmitted the sound well.

4 Repeat each test to give you more reliable results.

Material	Correct word heard
glass window	✓

5 Which materials did you find transmit sound well?

6 Which materials did you find do not transmit sound well?

What happens to sound under water?

Sound travels up to five times faster under water than in air. We hear the sound differently because the sound moves differently in water compared to air.

Our ears become filled with water and so the vibrations in our ears are different.

Be a scientist

A prediction is not a guess. Scientists make predictions based on their research or the results other scientists have collected.

▶ page 7

Have you ever swum under water? Describe to your partner how the sounds were different.

■ For more activities, go to Workbook 4 page 124.

We can use this knowledge to make quiet sounds seem different.

How does water change the way we hear sound?

1 Gently blow over the neck of an empty bottle. Can you make a sound?

   The air from you is vibrating the air in the bottle. This is vibrating the air back into your ears.

2 Add some water to your bottle and gently blow over the neck like you did before.

   What happens to the sound now?

3 Add different amounts of water and investigate the sounds you make.

4 Is there a pattern?

5 What do you conclude from your investigation? Think about the choices in these sentences to help you:

   When I added more water the volume of the sound *got louder* / *got quieter* / *stayed the same* and the sound *got higher* / *lower*.

Stretch zone

Why do some materials transmit sound better than others?

Hint: Think about what you know about particles in different materials.

Key idea

Sounds change when they travel through different materials.

■ For more activities, go to Workbook 4 page 125.

How can we make sounds louder?

In this lesson you will investigate how we can make sound travel better to our ears.

Key words

loud

transmit

vibration

Does distance make sounds fainter?

Can you make a tuning fork sound louder?

1 Hit the fork on a hard surface and hold it in the air. Listen to the sound it makes.

2 What happens to the sound when you move further away from the tuning fork?

   Is it louder or fainter?

3 Walk five metres away from the tuning fork and record your observations. Repeat your observations every five metres until you are 20 metres away.

4 Copy the table and record your observations.

Distance from tuning fork (m)	Observation
5	the sound was fainter/louder than next to the tuning fork

5 Write a conclusion about your investigation.

Be a scientist

Scientists try to make sense of their results by writing conclusions. Look at the investigation question to help you.

▶ page 13

■ For more activities, go to Workbook 4 page 126.

Make a telephone

Make a telephone from two paper cups and a long piece of string.

Can you hear your partner speak?
Can you hear them whisper?

This is how the telephone works:

1 Your voice causes waves. These vibrate the air particles.

2 The vibrating air particles make your cup vibrate.

3 The vibrations from the cup vibrate the string.

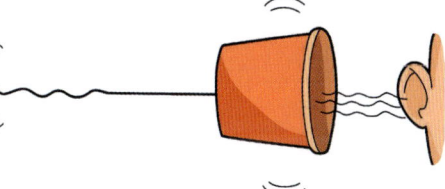

4 The vibrations from the string vibrate your partner's cup.

5 The cup vibrates the air, then your partner's ear drum.

Can you make your telephone work better?

1 Think about how well your string telephone worked. Try to change various things to make it a better device. You could change:
  - the type of string
  - the length of the string
  - how tight the string is
  - how big the cups are.

2 Which changes made your telephone better? Record your results.

Be a scientist

Scientists and engineers test devices and then try to make them better.
▶ page 13

Key idea
- Sounds are fainter if we move away from the source of the sound.
- We can make sound travel further with the right equipment.

■ For more activities, go to Workbook 4 page 127.

Some materials stop sound travelling

In this lesson you will investigate how some materials prevent sound from travelling through them.

Key words
ear defender
insulator

Think back

What are decibels? How loud would a sound of 10 dB be?

An aeroplane taking off has a sound-meter reading of 140 dB. Sounds of over 130 dB hurt our ears and sounds of 160 dB cause permanent damage.

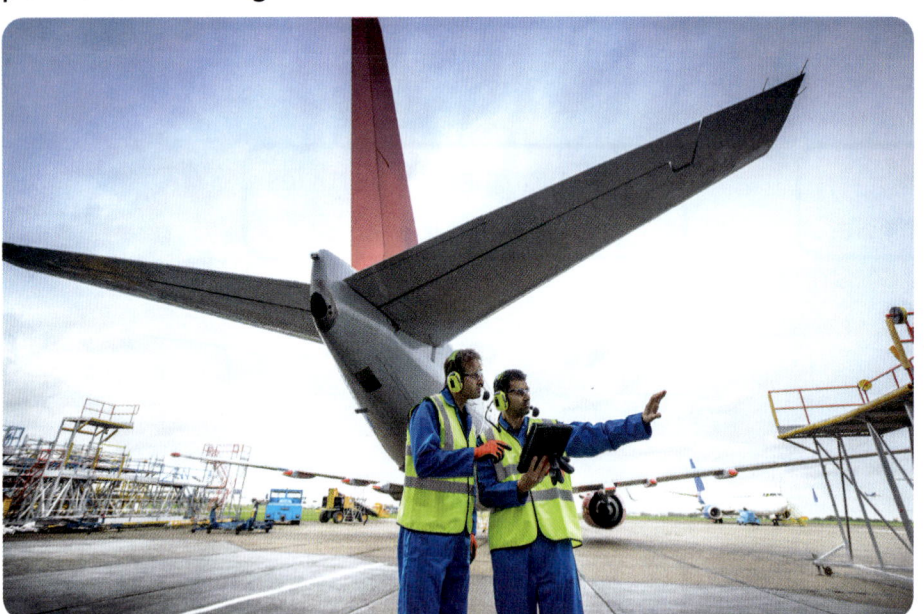

How are the people in the photograph protecting their ears?

Some materials are better at transmitting sound than others. To prevent damage to our ears from loud noises we use materials that are not good at transmitting vibrations.

Which material makes the best ear defenders?

You will need a radio, a box and some materials to test.

1 Switch on the radio and place it in the box. Can you hear the radio?

2 Wrap the box in each material and take a sound-level meter reading.

   If you do not have a sound-level meter, use a scale of 1 to 10 for how well you can hear the radio.

What piece of equipment could you use to measure the sound?

 For more activities, go to Workbook 4 page 128.

3 Copy the table and record your results.

Material	Sound level recorded (dB)
cotton wool	60 dB

4 Use your results to help you design some ear defenders.

Use these questions to help you think about your design.

- Which material will you use for your ear defenders?
- Which material would make the worst ear defenders?
- Can you explain why?

Materials that are not good at transmitting sounds are sound insulators. Sound insulation is not just used for ear defenders. Recording studios use insulation to prevent sound from outside travelling into the studio.

Curtains, carpets and rugs are good insulators of sound. Some studios put carpet and rugs on the walls.

You have now seen how sound insulators are used to stop sound travelling, in order to protect our ears and make life more comfortable.

Have you ever seen the wall inside a cinema?

Imagine what it would be like living next to a cinema without insulated walls.

Key idea

We can use some materials to protect our ears from very loud sounds.

Stretch zone

Can you think of any other uses of sound insulation?

■ For more activities, go to Workbook 4 page 129.

Investigating wave patterns of sound

In this lesson you will investigate how high or low a sound is (pitch) and that high and low sounds can be loud or quiet (volume).

Key words
loud
pattern
pitch
volume

Listen to a piece of music.

How many different sounds can you hear?

What is the highest note you can sing?

The pitch of a sound is how high or low it is.

How can we change the pitch of a sound?

Try the investigation from page 118 with a ruler again.

1 Start with a long length of ruler vibrating.

Is the pitch of the sound high or low?

2 Now hold the ruler so that only a small part of it vibrates.

Is the pitch higher or lower?

3 Use your guitar from page 119 to explore pitch. Change the length of a string by holding it down with one finger. Then pluck the string.

4 Make the string longer and shorter and listen to what happens to the pitch. Can you recognise a pattern?

5 Write down your conclusions about pitch and the length of the string.

An oscilloscope shows both the pitch and the volume of a sound. It shows this as a wave pattern. Remember that the volume can also be described as how quiet or loud a sound is.

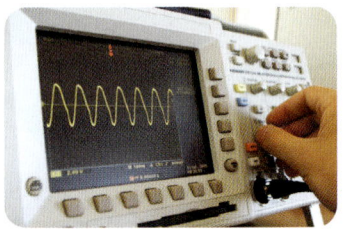

■ For more activities, go to Workbook 4 page 130.

The girls are measuring the volume and pitch of their voices. The microphone picks up the vibrations from their voices. The oscilloscope turns the vibrations into a wave pattern on the screen.

The number of waves tells us the pitch of a sound.

- In diagrams 1 and 2 there are only two waves. These waves are made by low-pitched sounds.
- In diagram 3 there are four waves. These waves are made by a high-pitched sound.

The height of the waves tells us how loud a sound is.

- In diagrams 2 and 3 the waves are high. These waves are made by loud sounds.
- In diagram 1 the waves are not as high. These waves are made by a quieter sound.

Investigating wave patterns

Look at these wave patterns from an oscilloscope.

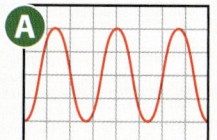 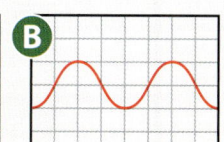 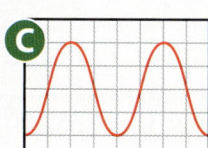 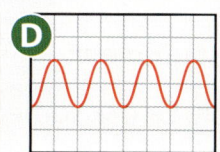

1 Which two are the loudest sounds?

2 Which sound has the highest pitch?

Key idea

Wave patterns can tell us about the pitch and volume of sounds.

5 Sounds

131

■ For more activities, go to Workbook 4 page 131.

Investigating the volume of sounds

In this lesson you will investigate how changes in volume of sounds are because of the energy in the vibrations.

Key words
amplify
pattern
vibration
volume

Think back

What is the link between energy and the size of vibrations it causes? How does this link to the loudness of a sound?

Whisper a word as quietly as you can to your partner. Did they hear the word?

Make a tambourine and investigate how to play it quietly or loudly

1 Use string to attach bells or shells to a paper plate, to make a tambourine.

2 Hold the tambourine and gently tap the centre.

   How would you describe the sound? Use the words 'pitch' and 'volume' in your description.

3 Now hit it harder.

   What happens to the volume of the sound?

Air is a good transmitter of sound. If you can force or push air particles together, sound travels even better. This makes the sound louder to our ears. Amplify means to make the sound louder. We will investigate this.

How can we amplify sound?

1 Blow up a balloon.

2 Place the balloon against your ear.

3 Gently tap on the balloon. Or ask someone to whisper into the balloon.

4 How loud is the sound?

■ For more activities, go to Workbook 4 page 132.

The tapping sounds very loud. This is called amplification.

When you blow the balloon up you force air particles into the balloon. The particles of air are squashed together very closely. The vibration from your tapping can move through the balloon very easily and carry the vibration to your ear.

When you whispered to your partner, did you cup your hands around your mouth? Why do you think we do this?

 Ear cones can amplify sound

1 Make an ear cone like the one in the picture.

2 Listen to some music. First with just your ears. Then with one cupped hand. Then with two cupped hands. Finally use your ear cone.

3 Write up your conclusions about listening to music in different ways.

Which technique makes the sound louder? Explain why this happens.

Science fact

In the past, people used to use cones to help them hear. Now they can use electronic hearing aids.

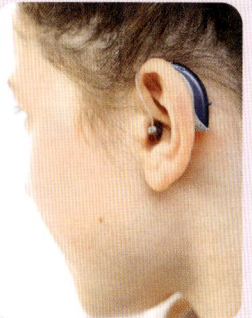

Key idea

We can make sounds louder by putting in more energy and directing the vibrations or waves towards our ears.

5 Sounds

133

■ For more activities, go to Workbook 4 page 133.

Making music

In this lesson you will explore how we can change pitch to make music.

Key words

music

pitch

Think back

How does changing the length of a vibrating object change the pitch?

Talk about the musical instruments you have made.

How did you change the pitch of the guitar you made?

When there was a small amount of ruler vibrating, the pitch was much higher. We shortened the guitar string by pressing a finger on the string.

In all instruments, if we can change the size of the object vibrating, we can change the pitch.

When musicians play a string instrument, like a guitar, they press on the string to change the length. This changes the pitch and makes a tune.

How do you think we can change the pitch of a drum?

 ### Making a musical instrument with bottles

Bottles make good instruments. We investigated blowing on bottles. When we add water to the bottle the pitch changes. This is because there is less air to vibrate.

1 Fill bottles to different levels.

2 See if you can make a tune.

■ For more activities, go to Workbook 4 page 134.

Making music with bottles

1 Tap an empty glass bottle with a stick. The vibration from the stick goes into the air in the bottle and makes a sound.

2 Set up five bottles and add different amounts of water to each.

3 Try to make a tune.

What do you think will happen to the pitch if you add some water? Test your prediction by carrying out the investigation.

Making pan flutes

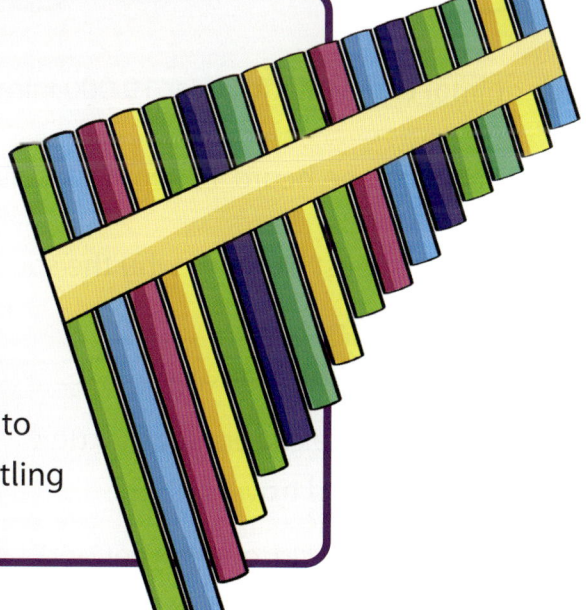

1 Line up about 16 straws.

2 Cut the straws to different lengths to make a pan flute. Use the picture to help you.

3 Use sticky tape to hold the straws together.

4 Practise blowing through the straws to make higher and lower pitched whistling sounds.

You could make an orchestra in your group.

Check how much you know.
Try the questions on pages 136–137.

Key idea

We can use changes in pitch to make music.

5 Sounds

135

■ For more activities, go to Workbook 4 page 135.

What have I learned about sounds?

1 What happens to the particles in the air as sound travels?

The particles v__ __ __ __ __ __

2 Circle the correct word to complete the sentence.

The further you move away from a source of sound, the **louder / fainter** the sound is.

3 Tick the correct ending for this sentence.

The pitch of sound is   how loud or faint it is. ☐

                  how high or low it is. ☐

4 Look at the pictures.

A

B

a Which animal can be heard over 10 000 kilometres away? _____

b Which animal can be heard 10 kilometres away? _____

c Which statement best explains why the sounds travel such different distances?
Tick the correct one.

One animal is shouting louder. ☐

Particles in the air are closer together and
so sounds vibrate and travel better. ☐

Particles in water are closer together and
so sounds vibrate and travel better. ☐

5 **a** The particles in some materials stop sound travelling. Circle the materials that are
good insulators.

bricks   bubble wrap   cardboard   carpet   curtains

foam   glass   metal   plastic   wood

■ For more activities, go to Workbook 4 page 136.

b Explain how an insulator is being used to protect the engineer's ears in the photo.

_____

_____

_____

6 Write these sounds in the correct box in the table.

child screaming   jet taking off   whisper

Sound	Sound level (dB)
	20
	110
	140

7 a Which oscilloscope wave pattern shows the highest pitched sound? _____

b Which shows the highest volume sound? _____

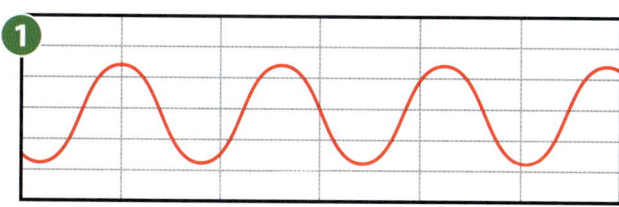

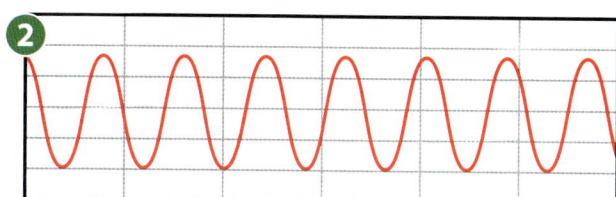

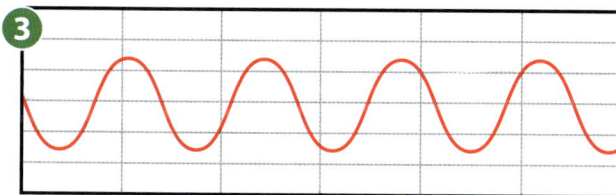

■ For more activities, go to Workbook 4 page 137.

Glossary

appliance

battery

bulb

buzzer

carnivore

circuit

component

condensation

conductor

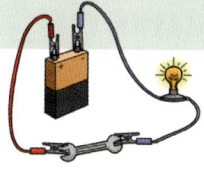

consumer

decibel

digestive system

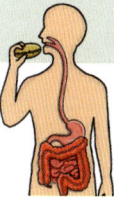

electricity

environment

evaporation

flowering plant

food chain

freezing

gas

habitat

herbivore

identification key

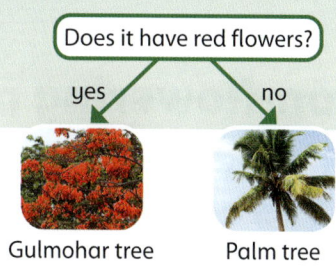

Gulmohar tree   Palm tree

insulator

invertebrate

liquid

loud

melting

natural disaster

non-flowering plant

omnivore

pattern

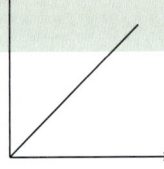

pitch

pollution

predator

prey

producer

quiet

solid

sound

switch

taste

teeth

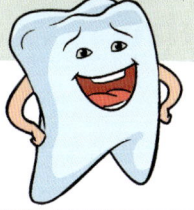

temperature

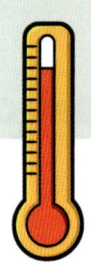

travel

vertebrate

vibrate

volume

water cycle

wire